The Windlesham/Rampton Report

The Windlesham/Rampton Report on
Death on the Rock

faber and faber
LONDON · BOSTON

First published in 1989
by Faber and Faber Limited
3 Queen Square London WC1N 3AU

Photoset by Parker Typesetting Service Leicester

Printed in Great Britain by
Richard Clay Ltd Bungay Suffolk

A CIP record for this book
is available from the British Library
ISBN 0-571-14150-1

Death on the Rock
was produced by Thames Television
and transmitted on 28 April 1988

Contents

Foreword by Sir Ian Trethowan
Chairman, Thames Television

'Death on the Rock' was not the first television programme concerned with Irish terrorism to have provoked acute controversy, nor will it be the last. Why, then, did Thames Television take the unprecedented step of commissioning an independent inquiry into its making and screening?

The attacks on the programme by some politicians, and by sections of the press, were at fault, and in some respects unscrupulous, but this was not in itself sufficient to call for an inquiry. What influenced us were indications that criticism spread beyond the familiar circle of habitual critics of television.

An opinion poll showed the public evenly divided, and some critics clearly felt a sense of outrage at any questioning of the shooting of three terrorists who were planning an act of terrible violence.

We were also influenced by the source of the Government's original initiative to stop the programme. Sir Geoffrey Howe has always been fair and reasonable in his dealings with the media, yet on this occasion it was he who led the Government's call for the programme to be postponed, and when the IBA turned down his request, he protested with unusual vehemence. As emerges from the report, while the IBA were justified in allowing the programme to be broadcast, the issues which Sir Geoffrey raised were important and complex, worthy of careful study in advance of any similar cases in the future.

Then there was the issue of credibility. Once Kenneth Asquez had repudiated the statement broadcast by Thames, some investigation was clearly desirable. The senior management of Thames would have been perfectly capable of carrying out a thorough and balanced inquiry, but in the highly charged atmosphere of the time it would not have carried sufficient credibility.

A further factor in our minds was the need for the inquiry to be conducted by people with enough authority to secure access to all the relevant evidence. Thames management might well have found some doors shut to them. An inquiry headed by a Privy Councillor and a QC was more likely to gain the co-operation of anyone who might have something to contribute.

So it proved. The report, as a result, is well-informed and conspicuously fair to the various interests involved. Even those who were hoping for a different outcome cannot dispute that Lord Windlesham and Mr Rampton have been painstakingly thorough in their investigations, and I believe that their analysis could prove of seminal importance to the future relationship between public authorities and the broadcasters.

The setting up of the inquiry alarmed some journalists. They felt it set a dangerous precedent. Even if the inquiry cleared the Thames programme-makers, would not television journalists be made more wary about venturing into similarly turbulent waters?

I understand this concern, but I do not share it. Television journalists are given the privilege of using the most far-reaching medium of communication devised by man. It is an awesome responsibility, and they must accept that the institutions and individuals whose affairs they seek to report, and the viewers who seek information from them, will be concerned about how they exercise that responsibility.

'Death on the Rock' dealt with highly controversial issues, and if the team was at fault, that fact should be publicly acknowledged and the appropriate conclusions drawn. If, on the other hand, the inquiry found that the programme was a legitimate piece of journalism, then that should be a reassurance to television journalists that, if they conducted themselves with professional integrity, they could address the most sensitive issues.

23 January 1989

Chapter One

The Inquiry
I: its scope and origins

1   On the afternoon of Sunday, 6 March 1988 two men and a woman were shot dead by security forces in the streets of Gibraltar. The IRA claimed all three as members of a unit on active service. The following day the Foreign Secretary, Sir Geoffrey Howe, informed the House of Commons of a plan to carry out an act of terrorism aimed at the weekly guard-mounting ceremony by the Royal Anglian Regiment. Had a bomb been exploded in the area where 50 soldiers normally assembled before the parade, not only they but a large number of civilians might have been killed or injured, with total potential casualties estimated as running into three figures. The Foreign Secretary said that the terrorists had been challenged by the security forces, and when challenged had made movements which led the military personnel operating in support of the Gibraltar police to conclude that their own lives and the lives of others were under threat. In the light of this response they had been shot. It was subsequently established that those killed were not carrying arms. A parked car in which one of them had entered Gibraltar earlier in the day was dealt with by a bomb disposal team after the shootings, and was found to contain no explosive device. Two days later approximately 64 kg of Semtex explosives, together with detonating equipment and 2 kg of ammunition, was found by Spanish police in another car left in a car park at Marbella. In his statement on 7 March the Foreign Secretary announced that an inquest would be held in Gibraltar.

2   The fatal incident was reported extensively in the British press and broadcast media as well as in Gibraltar and Spain. Eye-witnesses gave their accounts first to the local press and Gibraltar Broadcasting (GBC), and soon afterwards to the representatives of the British media when they arrived on the Rock. More

details of the operation were sought and alternative explanations aired. Several commentators expressed an implied or explicit suspicion that the IRA team had been shot by the SAS when they could have been arrested. Others went further, raising a possibility, in Enoch Powell's words, that the security forces might have committed 'deliberate, cold-blooded, premeditated murder'. (*Independent* 1 April 1988).

3 On Thursday, 28 April the Gibraltar shootings were the subject of a THIS WEEK special, produced by Thames Television and shown on all stations of the ITV network between 9:00–9:45 pm. The programme, entitled 'Death on the Rock', was extended from the usual running time of 26 minutes to 43 minutes because of the significance and topicality of the subject and the amount of material that had been gathered during seven weeks' intensive preparation. A detailed account of the making of the programme is contained in chapters Three, Six, Seven and Eight of this report; and the transcript is included as chapter Four. On the day of transmission the Independent Broadcasting Authority (IBA) rejected a personal request made by the Foreign Secretary on 26 April to postpone the showing of the programme until after the inquest had taken place. The correspondence between Sir Geoffrey Howe and Lord Thomson of Monifieth is published in chapter Eleven. Neither the programme management nor the Board of Thames were aware of this intervention until a press conference called by the Foreign Office at lunchtime on 28 April. No storm signals had previously been received by Thames, despite the fact that the plans for the programme had been known to the Ministry of Defence for some weeks.

4 A selection of headlines in the national press on 29 April give the flavour of the controversy which followed: 'Trial by TV' row over IRA killings film (*The Times*), Defiant ITV angers Ministers as plea on SAS film is rejected (*Daily Telegraph*), IBA rejects government gag attempt (*Guardian*), Storm at SAS Telly Trial (*Sun*), Fury over SAS 'Trial by TV' (*Daily Mail*), TV Slur on the

SAS (*Daily Star*). What were perceived as the rights and wrongs of the editorial stance taken in the programme, and the decision to broadcast it, continued to be debated heatedly inside and outside Parliament for several weeks. Strongly felt criticisms were made and widely publicized, while the programme was defended by those who believed it exposed disturbing questions that should be pursued by way of a judicial inquiry.

5 Then, on 23 September, as the furore was dying down, a totally unexpected development occurred on the fourteenth day of the inquest at Gibraltar. A young man, who had made a statement to a lawyer which had been used in the programme, withdrew it, saying that he had been pressured into giving an untrue account of what he had seen to an intermediary acting for THIS WEEK. As a result of his contradictory evidence the IBA, which had stood by the programme throughout the controversy, discussed with Thames the need for some form of investigation into the way it had been made. At first an internal inquiry was envisaged, but the IBA was not persuaded this would carry sufficient public confidence. After further exchanges, in which it was pointed out that the IBA would have to satisfy itself as regards the performance of the programme company in complying with its contractual obligations, Thames decided upon a full inquiry by two independent persons unconnected either with the Company or the Authority.

6 On 5 October 1988, Lord Windlesham accepted an invitation from the Board of Thames 'to conduct an Inquiry into the making and screening of "Death on the Rock"', to be joined by a senior lawyer. On 11 October Richard Rampton, QC was appointed to the Inquiry in this capacity. Work started immediately, with a public invitation being issued to anyone who wished to submit information relevant to the scope of the Inquiry to contact its Secretary. On 17 October Manuel Barca, a barrister in private practice, joined the Inquiry as Secretary.

7 Our terms of reference were to inquire into the making and screening of 'Death on the Rock'. That has led us to examine, and reach conclusions about, the genesis, preparation, content and effect of the programme, and any impact which its broadcast might have had upon the subsequent inquest. From the outset, we have emphasized that it was no part of our remit to investigate the actual shootings which took place in Gibraltar on 6 March, still less to draw conclusions about what happened or the reasons why it happened. The inquest shed light on some of the disputed questions of fact which we have had to consider, and consequently we have studied carefully the coroner's summing-up and much of the evidence which was given. Nothing in this report should be taken as putting a gloss on the proceedings or the verdict returned at the inquest which are described in chapter Nine, paragraphs 135–136. Many people still hold firm opinions about the Gibraltar shootings, and we hope they may resist the temptation to draw on our report selectively to reinforce existing beliefs. It needs to be read as a whole.

8 We were conscious that in undertaking a detailed scrutiny of a single television programme, with a view to producing a published report, we were embarking on uncharted waters. Not only did we lack any powers to secure the co-operation of those whom we wished to hear from, but we were anxious to ensure that anyone whom we interviewed was fairly treated. This meant devising procedures which would allow all of the interested parties a proper opportunity of dealing with any matters which might be regarded as adverse to them. To this end we provided, wherever possible, advance lists of questions which we intended to raise, with particular reference to aspects on which those interviewed might be vulnerable to criticism. In oral interviews we brought forward any potential criticisms of weight in order to provide an opportunity to answer them. We agreed to legal representation, and one journalist was accompanied by his solicitor when he met us. Meetings with the IBA and the Ministry of Defence were also attended by their legal advisers. As we drafted the report we provided opportunities for those affected

by provisional conclusions to comment and for their lawyers to make written submissions. The National Union of Journalists (NUJ) and two firms of solicitors made representations on the form of the Inquiry, and we acknowledge their assistance in helping us to evolve the procedures described in this paragraph.

9 It needs to be said that while co-operating with the Inquiry, the NUJ told us plainly that it wished to:

'place on record its firm belief that it sees no need for any inquiry such as the one currently taking place. Such a development is a retrograde step for journalism in this country.

'There are procedures and institutions already in existence to deal with any alleged journalistic abuses or mistakes, such as the NUJ's own Ethics Council, the Press Council or the Broadcasting Complaints Commission.

'We believe the inquiry was set up as a result of political pressure and is a method of harassment of journalists who are involved in the type of journalism which poses awkward issues.'

10 With this reservation, which was the only one of its kind made to us, almost all of the parties directly concerned with the matters examined in our Inquiry co-operated fully, and we thank them for the time and care with which written submissions were prepared, supplemented in certain cases by oral interviews. We have tried to avoid being too legalistic in our language and procedures wherever possible, especially as references to witnesses and evidence could lead to confusion with witnesses to the shootings, some of whom later appeared in the film and/or gave evidence at the Gibraltar inquest.

11 We received written or oral submissions and comments from those listed below. Where an oral interview took place it is marked by an asterisk.

Thames Television

* Sir Ian Trethowan (Chairman)
* Richard Dunn (Managing Director)
* David Elstein (Director of Programmes)
* Barrie Sales (Deputy Director of Programmes and Director of News and Current Affairs)
* Roger Bolton (Editor, THIS WEEK)
* Christopher Oxley (Producer, 'Death on the Rock')
* Julian Manyon (Reporter, 'Death on the Rock') accompanied by P. M. Raphael and Joanne Rickards (Peters & Peters, Solicitors)
* Alison Cahn (Researcher, 'Death on the Rock')
  Louise Hayman (Programme Legal Adviser/Executive Assistant to the Managing Director)

Independent Broadcasting Authority

* Lord Thomson of Monifieth (Chairman)
* John Whitney (Director General)
* David Glencross (Director of Television)
* Kenneth Blyth (Secretary)
* David Kemp, QC
* John Rink and John O'Conor (Allen and Overy, Solicitors)

Foreign and Commonwealth Office

Sir Patrick Wright (Permanent Under-Secretary of State)
Sir John Fretwell (Deputy to the Permanent Under-Secretary of State and Political Director)

Ministry of Defence

K. C. Macdonald (Second Permanent Under-Secretary of State)
* An Assistant Under-Secretary of State, accompanied by the Director of Public Relations, Army, a Legal Adviser, and a

member of the General Staff Secretariat, gave oral evidence to the Inquiry supplementing written submissions.

Gibraltar

* Mr and Mrs M. Proetta
* Stephen Bullock
* Douglas Celecia
* Major R. Randall
* Christopher Finch

Others

* Lieutenant-Colonel George Styles GC
* H. Conroy (General Secretary) and J. Foster (National Broadcasting Organizer), National Union of Journalists
  David Miller (Department of Sociology, University of Glasgow)
  June Tweedie (INQUEST: United Campaigns for Justice)
  T. P. O'Malley (Administrator, Campaign for Press and Broadcasting Freedom)
  Antony Whitaker (Legal Manager, Times Newspapers Limited)
  Robin Morgan (Features Editor, *Sunday Times*)
  Rosie Waterhouse (ex-Insight reporter, *Sunday Times*)

12 We also wish to acknowledge the assistance given to the Inquiry by the following:
Air Chief Marshal Sir Peter Terry (Governor of Gibraltar)
The Hon Mr Justice Kneller (Chief Justice of Gibraltar)
Eric Thistlethwaite, QC (Attorney-General of Gibraltar)
J. L. Canepa (Commissioner of Police, Gibraltar)
Sir Joshua Hassan, QC (J. A. Hassan and Partners)
Lord Nicholas Gordon-Lennox (HM Ambassador in Madrid)
Sr Don José J. Puig de la Bellacasa (Spanish Ambassador in London)
Sr Don José I. Carbajal (Minister/Counsellor, Spanish Embassy)

Sir Geoffrey Cox
Jonathan Dimbleby
Sir Denis Forman
Richard Francis
Jeremy Isaacs
Peters & Peters, Solicitors
Clarke Willmott & Clarke, Solicitors

Chapter Two

The Inquiry
II: the context

13 Before moving on to an account of how 'Death on the Rock' was made, and attempting an assessment of its true meaning and effect, issues which go to the heart of the Inquiry, we set the programme in the context of current affairs reporting on television as a whole. To do otherwise would be to subject a particular programme to rigorous scrutiny in isolation, without an appreciation of the factors which bear upon the presentation of news and current affairs and the justification for them.

14 We start with the proposition that the freedom of the press and broadcast media is an integral part of a free society. The degree of freedom and the pressures upon it will always be contentious, but the principle should be beyond challenge that the public interest is advanced 'by publishing the facts and opinions without which a democratic electorate cannot make responsible judgements'. (Royal Commission on the Press, *Final Report*, 1977, Cmnd 6810 pp 8–9). That said, the freedom to examine and report on issues of public importance carries with it a corresponding responsibility. Inaccurate or unfair reporting may cause injustice and distress to those who are its victims, while doing a disservice to society generally. The public may be misled into making false judgements, and the realization that an apparently serious exposition of an issue is flawed in point of fairness or accuracy may undermine trust in the press or broadcasting as reliable media of communication.

15 From the earliest days of broadcasting, first radio and then television adopted and have largely maintained the traditions of press freedom. There are significant differences, however, originating from the scarcity of radio frequencies allocated by the State. The most important of these is the specific obligation

to be fair and unbiased in the presentation of news and current affairs. So the journalists working on these programmes are not free agents. In Independent Television they are subject to a regulatory framework made up both of statutory and conventional requirements. Section 4(1)(f) of the Broadcasting Act 1981, re-enacting earlier legislation, calls for due impartiality on the part of persons providing programmes on matters of political or industrial controversy or relating to public policy. Responsibility for ensuring compliance rests with the IBA which has a duty placed on it by Parliament to satisfy itself as far as possible that the content of any programmes supplied for transmission by a programme contractor fulfils the requirements of the Broadcasting Act. The IBA does not seek to intervene directly in the production process, seeing its role more as controlling the programme company than the production staff.

16 As a guide to good practice the IBA periodically publishes guidelines which include a section on fairness and impartiality in current affairs and documentary programmes (*Television Programme Guidelines*, IBA, April 1985, Section 6.3). The guidelines make clear that whereas the notion of balance is not to be interpreted in any simple mathematical sense as being equal time for the expression of opposing viewpoints, nevertheless programmes should not be slanted by the concealment of relevant facts, or by misleading emphasis; nor should investigation turn into a case for the prosecution or defence, or into a form of trial by television. Programme companies may also have their own guidelines specifying the practices and standards expected of the journalists and other programme producers in their employ. We are not concerned in this report with the BBC, but there too the requirements of the Royal Charter and Licence and Agreement are interpreted and enforced by a public corporation.

17 Consequently broadcast journalism is more closely regulated than is print journalism. All forms of journalism are subject to the general law of defamation, contempt, confidentiality, copyright and official secrets. Aside from that, print journalism is subject to

no special legal constraints. The Press Council is a voluntary, not a statutory, body which can investigate and upbraid those who fall short of the standards it expects, but it has no further sanctions. The IBA on the contrary has a battery of legal powers of enforcement. It can withhold or postpone transmission of any programme offered by a programme company if it is not satisfied that it complies with the requirements of the Broadcasting Act or the *Television Programme Guidelines*. After transmission, the IBA may call for an apology on screen, or make a reprimand. As a final sanction, it can issue a notice of breach of contract. The Broadcasting Complaints Commission (BCC), another statutory body, has a narrower remit. It considers complaints of unjust or unfair treatment or of unwarranted infringements of privacy. Complaints must be made in writing and the complainant must have had a direct interest in the subject matter of the broadcast. The BCC has a statutory power to compel the broadcaster to broadcast a summary of its findings, or to publish that summary in the relevant programme journal.

18 In addition to the requirements of the IBA and their employers, broadcast journalists subscribe to a code of values and professional standards. Since the process of producing a television programme is a collaborative one, the prevailing climate of what is or is not accepted as proper journalistic practice is crucial. The relevant principle is expressed in the NUJ's *Code of Professional Conduct*:

'3. A journalist shall strive to ensure that the information he/she disseminates is fair and accurate, avoid the expression of comment and conjecture as established fact and falsification by distortion, selection or misrepresentation.'

19 The ideal of objectivity is an elusive one, perhaps incapable of achievement in view of the reality that it depends on contrasting values and judgements. But its pursuit is enduringly worthwhile and lies behind the requirements of balance, fairness and the avoidance of bias which we have outlined. Easily as these virtues

roll off the tongue, and sincere as the disposition to act accordingly may be, nevertheless the lack of scruple of the few may call in question the bona fides of the many. Broadcast journalism has to guard against becoming a closed world of its own, a privileged fraternity determining for itself objectives and standards, and rejecting outside criticism as ill-informed or motivated by self-interest. In his 1988 Fleming Memorial Lecture John Birt, Deputy Director-General of the BBC, spoke trenchantly about the need for open-mindedness:

'The pursuit of accurate, impartial, fair and inquiring journalism of quality on television and elsewhere comes easiest to those who have open minds; a sense of humility about the permanence of understanding and the fluidity of circumstances and ideas; a respect for the complexity of problems and of their causes; a willingness to get out and about and to do some hard work. It comes hardest to those imbued with a disdain for, and not just a healthy suspicion of, established centres of power; and with a preference for pontificating rather than for discovery. Television needs more journalists with open minds.'

20 However scrupulous the adherence to the requirements of the common law, statute, contract and convention, these prescriptions cannot always provide a complete answer to the difficult questions which periodically arise as to whether a particular programme should be made, and, if so, what form it should take, and when it should be broadcast. There will be programmes which may satisfy all the requirements, but which still give rise to a conflict of public interests. One side of that conflict will be represented by the public interest in freedom of expression referred to in paragraph 14. The competing interest may take a variety of forms. The problem which arises in such cases cannot, *ex hypothesi*, be resolved by reference to established legal or conventional principles, but must in each case be a matter of judgement for, in the first place, the journalists who make the programmes; in the second place, for the company which employs them; and, lastly, for the broadcasting authority.

21 Whenever the government becomes involved in a dispute over the showing of a programme, conflicts of interest are likely to occur in the most acute form. To some, the mere fact that a Minister of the Crown requests a broadcasting organization not to transmit a programme, on the grounds that to do so would be injurious to the national interest, should be sufficient reason for compliance. Yet the national interest is no Holy Grail in the exclusive guardianship of the government of the day. Many other interests combine to constitute any adequate expression of national interest; and opinions differ, sometimes very strongly, on the weight which should be given to the varying strands. As we have argued, the freedom to publish is itself a fundamental and enduring part of the national interest. So too is the function of the press and broadcast media to act as a curb on the abuse of power or maladministration. All these things need to be put into the balance when a Minister intervenes. No one should attempt to deny his right to do so, nor his entitlement to expect a prompt and courteous response. The fact that such requests may be backed up by strenuous attempts to influence and persuade the broadcasters or the public of the merits of the government's case need occasion no surprise. At the end of the day, however, it is the responsible broadcasting organization, in ITV either the programme company Board or the IBA, which must decide. Other than in a limited number of instances, Parliament has not transferred that power, in effect the editorial control over what is broadcast, to Ministers. It is a responsibility that rests heavily on the shoulders of those who bear it, but that is where it properly belongs.

22 We offer this report, therefore, not as the product of an inquisition bent on restricting the rightful prerogative of the journalist to probe where he is not welcome and to ask awkward questions, but as a genuine attempt to see what can be learned from a detailed study of a programme about a contentious issue of high public importance which itself became the subject of intense controversy. Where we criticize we have attempted to do so in a constructive spirit, avoiding condemnation or obloquy. In this

connection, we draw attention to some words of warning by Lord Thomson in his valedictory lecture after eight years as IBA chairman:

'Broadcasters, as any chairman of a broadcasting authority has reason to know, are often their own worst enemies. One of the cardinal temptations for them in both current affairs and cultural broadcasting is a certain arrogance, and an extraordinary sensitivity if anyone questions their freedom to do things exactly in their own way. Broadcasters, who spend their lives critically cross-examining Ministers and MP's are curiously sensitive when it comes to being criticized themselves.'

23 Throughout our deliberations we have had in mind the dangers of hindsight. 'Death on the Rock' was transmitted in April 1988, over four months before the inquest opened in Gibraltar, and more than five months before the setting-up of our Inquiry. The programme was made without the co-operation of the Ministry of Defence which declined to comment on the shootings until the inquest. On each of the contested issues we have aimed at reaching a conclusion on whether the stance taken in the programme was justified in the light of the information which was, or could have been, available at the time.

Chapter Three

The programme and the programme-makers

24 For more than 30 years the THIS WEEK programme has been a mainstay of the ITV schedule. Launched as a weekly news magazine by Associated-Rediffusion in 1956, it was inherited by Thames Television on taking over as the London weekday contractor in 1967. In 1978 the programme was re-named TV EYE and given a more popular brief, but in 1986 the original title and the stirring theme music from the Karelia Suite were re-introduced. For three decades the half-hour programmes have been shown simultaneously at peak viewing times by all companies making up the ITV national network, attracting audiences of between five and ten million viewers. Many highly regarded producers and reporters have worked on the series which has often been commended by the IBA. Of its diverse nature ITV has had more than one flagship, but THIS WEEK has been consistently in the forefront of its current affairs coverage.

25 Although aimed at a mass audience ('Death on the Rock' was estimated to have been seen by 6.5 million viewers), and contained in a schedule of programmes designed to entertain, amuse and relax as well as to inform, THIS WEEK has become progressively more journalistic in its approach over the years. While the visual properties of a current affairs programme contribute powerfully to the effect of the completed work in a way which is denied to print journalism and sound broadcasting, the ideas claim primacy. The journalistic function is performed by a team of programme editor, producer, reporter and researcher, who select the subjects, carry out the necessary research, find and interview the participants, decide upon the line and shape of the programme, and write and speak the commentary. It follows that the journalists, subject to the management to which they

are answerable, are primarily responsible for the fairness and accuracy of the programme and for the impression it will create in the minds of the viewing public. For this reason, rather than from any lack of appreciation of the importance of the technical and craft skills, we concentrate in this report on the work of the journalists in their capacity as programme-makers.

26 The reference to management throws into relief one of the most common, and profound, sources of friction in television. This stems from divergent notions of authorship and the role of management authority, each bringing with it a separate inter-pretation of responsibility. The reporter and producer may look at the programme, for entirely respectable reasons, as *their* programme; something which they have created and for which they are responsible. Once its main lines and the cost have been agreed, the content and presentation, on this argument, are matters for the programme-makers. At the same time, the direc-tors of the programme company, or executives with management roles within the organization, may regard the programme as something for which they have formal responsibilities, and hence look on it as being *their* programme. Friction of this kind exists elsewhere in those media which depend on managerial skills to bring creative work to fruition and public exhibition, such as the theatre and publishing. But because of its complex regulatory framework it is in television above all that the internal contradictions between the prerogatives of authorship and administration are fought out in contests where boundaries sel-dom remain in the same place for long.

27 From the start, THIS WEEK was intended to deal with topical issues, and politicians were not slow to make use of the oppor-tunities it offered. Eden, Macmillan, Gaitskell and Harold Wilson all appeared in the early days and, as the mobility of film crews increased, the programme's resources enabled it to cover a wider range of stories on location at home and overseas. Although from time to time at odds with Government or Opposition, THIS WEEK (or TV EYE) has remained the place

where the Prime Minister and other party leaders have often been interviewed at length on ITV. Since taking office in 1979, Mrs Thatcher has been interviewed for the full duration of the programme on five occasions, with shorter interviews during Party Conferences or General Election campaigns. Other editions deal with subjects of immediate topical interest, sometimes reactive (such as a programme shortly after the Piper Alpha disaster), but more often issue-based programmes taking a more analytical approach. The Editor of THIS WEEK told us that while there is no general agreement on what is regarded as investigative journalism, he estimated that about one in five programmes would fall within the category conventionally known as investigative. We regard 'Death on the Rock' as coming within this proportion.

28 In current affairs television, as in the press, there has been a noticeable growth in recent years in investigative reporting, based on the premise that the reality may be very different from outward appearances, especially where the appearances are perceived to result from what those in authority want the public to know and believe. Before committing expensive resources producers need to have a clear idea of a programme's purpose. Is it to expose wrong-doing, or it is to postulate questions that are capable of more than one answer? If the former, the ground needs to be thoroughly prepared in advance. If the latter, it is essential that the conclusion of the programme should not be decided upon before the questions are put and the answers considered. Confusion of purpose at this stage can lead to misunderstanding and recrimination later.

29 The viewer is entitled to expect that a programme which sets out to present questions should do so with an open mind. Investigative programmes of this sort may well eschew generalization and ask, pointedly if need be: How did this happen? Why did it happen? What precisely happened? What was the effect? Journalistic inquiries on these lines can contribute to a wider public understanding of issues. The more important the event,

the greater the legitimacy in posing such questions, unwelcome though they may be to some of those at whom they are directed. What is illegitimate, in fulfilling the journalists' obligation towards the audience, is to pre-determine the answers.

30   The genesis of 'Death on the Rock' lay in the shootings which took place in Gibraltar on Sunday, 6 March and the Foreign Secretary's statement in the House of Commons the following day. The Director of News and Current Affairs at Thames, Barrie Sales, told us that to his mind the Foreign Secretary's explanation raised more questions than it answered and that by Tuesday, 8 March 'there was a growing suspicion, reinforced by newspaper reports of eyewitness accounts that no warnings had been given, that the three terrorists had been virtually executed and that the security services had acted outside the law.' It seemed to Sales that the 'basic unresolved question at the heart of Sir Geoffrey Howe's statement was why three unarmed terrorists, when challenged by armed security personnel, should make suspicious movements, which gave the impression they were a threat? . . . It did not make sense; there was no logic to it.' The Editor of THIS WEEK, Roger Bolton, had already initiated some inquiries on the Monday morning and by the time he proposed the programme to Sales, the senior editorial executive to whom he was directly responsible, they were agreed there was sufficient potential for a THIS WEEK programme (see chapter Six, paragraph 64).

31   The two of them decided that because of the intrinsic importance of the incident and its possible repercussions in Northern Ireland, as well as the controversy in Parliament and the press over what had happened, a THIS WEEK team should be allocated to research the story in Gibraltar and Spain. The Editor had at his disposal six producers, five reporters and five researchers, normally working in teams consisting of a producer, a reporter and a researcher on each project. The average time spent on a project was approximately four weeks, and most of the staff employed by THIS WEEK contributed between five and

seven programmes a year. Typically they would also have worked on several other projects which would have been dropped after the preliminary research had been completed.

32 The only team relatively free at the time consisted of a reporter, Julian Manyon, and a producer, Christopher Oxley, who were preparing a programme on British Aerospace and the Japanese car industry and were on the point of leaving for Japan. Bolton considered them to be an experienced pairing with qualities balancing each other, and he switched them to the Gibraltar story. Two researchers (Eamon Hardy and Alison Cahn) supplemented the team at various times. On Tuesday, 8 March, Manyon left for Spain and Oxley for Gibraltar. By 14 March both had returned to London, and at an editorial discussion with Bolton the following day the decision was made to start filming, but with an understanding that it might be abandoned at a later stage. On 16 March Gibraltar first appeared on the forward-planning sheet issued weekly by Bolton and seen by Sales (who in addition to his editorial responsibilities was Deputy Director of Programmes) and David Elstein (the Director of Programmes and former Editor of THIS WEEK). Since May 1988 Richard Dunn, the Managing Director of Thames has also received the forward-planning sheet; but his name was not on the distribution list at the material time.

33 Although the setting for 'Death on the Rock' was Gibraltar and Spain, the connection with the Provisional IRA has caused us to inquire closely into any filming that took place in Northern Ireland. We find that a THIS WEEK unit visited the province twice in the course of the programme's production. The first occasion was on 16 March to cover the funeral in Belfast of the three terrorists who had been shot in Gibraltar. A short sequence of 45 seconds showing the crowded funeral procession was included in the completed programme. Manyon also took the opportunity of the presence of Gerry Adams, the President of Sinn Fein, to film an interview with him. During this interview Adams refused to confirm that the IRA had been planning

to bomb the Tuesday parade in Gibraltar. It was decided that to use the interview would give the IRA a propaganda platform that could not be justified. Accordingly none of it was included in the completed programme.

34 Before the notice issued to the IBA by the Home Secretary on 19 October 1988 under Section 29(3) of the Broadcasting Act 1981 restricting the broadcasting of statements by Northern Ireland terrorist organizations and their apologists, the Authority required all programmes relating to Northern Ireland or the IRA to comply with certain guidelines. Under the cumbrous heading *Interviews with people who use or advocate violence or other criminal measures* the guidelines state:

'Any plans for a programme item which explores and exposes the views of people who within the British Isles use or advocate violence or other criminal measures for the achievement of political ends must be referred to the IBA before any arrangements for filming or videotaping are made. A producer should therefore not plan to interview members of proscribed organisations, for example, members of the Provisional IRA or other para-military organisations, without previous discussion with his/her company's top management. The management, if they think the item may be justified, will then consult the IBA.

'In exceptional and unforeseen circumstances, it may be impossible for a news reporting team to consult before recording such an item.' (*Television Programme Guidelines*, Section 8.1(i).)

35 The Editor of THIS WEEK has told us that he did not consider he was required by the guidelines to notify the IBA of the filming in Belfast on 16 March, either before or after it had taken place. First, the funeral was a public event and not one specially set up for filming by THIS WEEK. The world's press and cameras were there, including those of ITN. Second, even if a THIS WEEK unit had not been present, ITN footage could have been used without consulting the IBA since by the time of the broadcast of 'Death on the Rock' the ITN coverage had already been shown on ITV without any restriction being placed on its re-use. Third, no permission was required at the time to record interviews with

members of Sinn Fein. We asked the IBA for their comments, and the Director of Television informed us that it had not been the practice to expect prior consultation before filming IRA funerals from ITN, Ulster Television or current affairs programmes, including THIS WEEK. Since Sinn Fein was not a proscribed organization the interview with Adams did not require prior notification.

36 Guidelines are more than a private communication between the IBA and the programme companies. They are a public declaration of how Independent Television handles sensitive matters of concern to the viewing audience. Guidelines on bad language, the portrayal of violence, sex and nudity, privacy, fairness and impartiality have all emerged over the years from discussion between the programme-makers and the broadcasting authority. Once they have been agreed, they should be clearly expressed and widely promulgated. In fact, the guideline references to Northern Ireland are not easily found. They do not feature in the table of contents of the published *Television Programme Guidelines*, being included in the text under the general heading 'Crime, Anti-Social Behaviour, etc'. The wording of Section 8.1(i) is capable of more than one interpretation and, although it may now be water under the bridge, we would have entered a plea for thought to be given to drawing up a more accessible statement of practice in such a crucially important area of programme-making.

37 The consultative process between Thames and the IBA did not begin until the end of March. The initial contact between Bolton and the IBA's Programme Officer took the form of an informal talk when they met at a dinner on 29 March. Bolton confirmed there were no plans for secret filming or interviews with members of proscribed organizations, and said that when there was a definite transmission date and he had a better idea of how the programme would turn out he would get back to the IBA. He was told the IBA would almost certainly want to preview the programme.

38 As the production progressed, other elements were contem-
plated and discarded. So as to bring home to the viewers as
dramatically as possible the catastrophic effects had a bomb
been successfully exploded in the crowded streets of Gibraltar,
Bolton had conceived the idea of filming a controlled detonation
similar in destructive power to the quantity of explosives found
in the car in Spain. No private contractor would do this without
the consent and co-operation of the Ministry of Defence which,
after lengthy negotiation, was not forthcoming. Bolton persisted
with his determination to demonstrate the terrible consequences
of IRA violence, especially as it had become evident during the
team's research that in all probability the IRA had begun
planning the Gibraltar operation before the outrage at the
Remembrance Sunday parade in Enniskillen on 8 November
1987 when the explosion of a far smaller bomb had killed 11
people and wounded more than 50.

39 Once the filming in Gibraltar had been completed, the team
returned again to Northern Ireland, this time to Enniskillen,
where Manyon obtained a moving interview, beside her
husband's hospital bed, with the wife of a gravely injured
survivor still in a coma as a result of the blast. Partly to
accommodate this material, Bolton sought a dispensation for the
programme to be extended beyond its standard duration of
25–26 minutes. On 31 March, Elstein (the Director of
Programmes) agreed to support this proposal, and on 11 April
the Network Programme Controllers meeting agreed that
'Death on the Rock' should be scheduled to run for 43 minutes
49 seconds between 9:00–9:45 pm, with one centre break for
commercials, on Thursday, 28 April. As broadcast, the
sequence depicting the human tragedy caused by IRA bombings
lasted for little more than two minutes, although it made a
powerful impact early in the programme.

40 Shortly after transmission Mrs Noreen Hill, the wife of the
crippled hospital patient, was reported as feeling 'numb' and 'let
down' by the programme, saying that she and her husband had

been 'used to provide a piece of emotive footage for a documentary that discredited what the SAS had achieved in Gibraltar' (*Sunday Times* 8 May 1988). An Ulster Unionist Councillor from Enniskillen, Samuel Foster, who had helped the THIS WEEK team to set up the filming, had already sent a letter of complaint to Elstein on 2 May 1988. In forceful language he criticized 'Death on the Rock' for omitting an interview that had been filmed with a second victim of the blast, who had given a harrowing account of his experience. Councillor Foster claimed that the programme had concentrated on the accounts of people in Gibraltar (the eyewitnesses) who had no direct knowledge of terrorism, saying that he considered the programme to be 'disgustingly insulting and profoundly scornful of the innocents of the carnage in Enniskillen on Remembrance Day'. On 11 May Oxley replied on behalf of the Director of Programmes. Contrary to Councillor Foster's charge, he contended that 'Death on the Rock' had emphasized the potential for devastation in Gibraltar. His letter continued:

'No one could fail to have been moved by the image of Mrs Hill's vigil at her husband's bedside and the interview in which she displayed remarkable faith and fortitude.

'Indeed, such was the power of this sequence that we considered it could stand alone to display the true horrors of terrorism. Consequently, we decided not to use the interview with Mr and Mrs Dixon.

'I appreciate you may not have agreed with the examination of the shootings in Gibraltar but the methods by which the State deals with dangerous terrorists is a major issue, as the debate generated by our programme has proved.'

41 On 15 May the *Sunday Times* published a letter from Elstein in which he answered the previous week's critical article:

'We regret very much that Mrs Hill, the wife of one of the victims of Enniskillen, apparently was upset by the programme, but we deny that she was misled as you reported. Those who saw the film know that her husband's tragedy was legitimately presented in order to demonstrate the appalling and continuing consequences of terrorism and the hypocrisy of the IRA in claiming that Enniskillen was a "tragic mis-take", while at the same time planning a worse outrage in Gibraltar.'

Emotional reactions by those who had suffered such anguish as a result of the bombing in Enniskillen are entirely understandable. Feelings of extreme bitterness about the IRA coalesced with what was perceived as an unfair attack on the security forces which stood protectively between the terrorists and their inno-cent victims. Despite this criticism we are in no doubt that, when dispassionately viewed as an element in 'Death on the Rock', the sequence with Mrs Hill and her husband was a significant one which underlined the hostile editorial stance of the programme towards the IRA and its methods.

42 In Gibraltar the research entailed an extensive door-to-door canvass for eyewitnesses who were willing to be filmed. Some local people were apprehensive and reluctant to talk about what they had seen, either to the police or the press. The selection of those who were interviewed for the programme, and the use made of their interviews, is analysed in chapters Six, Seven and Eight. The possible implications in terms of prejudicing the inquest or contaminating the evidence are considered in chap-ters Nine and Ten.

43 There are two general points which can usefully be made at this stage. The first is that at the meeting with Manyon and Oxley on 15 March Bolton stressed that the production team needed to be very careful about who was paid for what, saying it should be made clear to all prospective interviewees in Gibraltar that THIS WEEK was not in the business of paying for interviews. One man, a taxi driver, who did not want to be identified, claimed to have a horrific account which he was only prepared to reveal if it was made worth his while. The researcher, Alison Cahn, checked with the producer, but Oxley confirmed that no payment should be made. When this reply was given it marked the end of the team's dealings with the man.

44 To our knowledge, only five Gibraltarians received payments from Thames for services in connection with the programme. They were: Major Randall, who was paid for the use of an extract from a video-recording made by him in the immediate aftermath of the shootings; Christopher Finch, a lawyer who received professional fees for legal services; two local journalists; and one photographer. We have seen copies of invoices for two amounts of £1000 which were paid to Randall. The first was for the rights in his video material which was included in the original broadcast on 28 April. This was at the rate of £400 per minute which Thames's Managing-Director has confirmed 'was in the normal range, albeit towards the upper end because of the unique nature of the material and its significance to the programme.' The agreement included the right to use the material for on-air promotion. Thames Television International later negotiated a second fee of the same amount to cover the residual rights when the programme was sold overseas. As regards the legal fees paid to Finch, we have been assured that they were in line with normal professional charges. Dominique Searle, a reporter on the *Gibraltar Chronicle* (and a stringer for the London *Times*), was paid £200 as a consultancy and research fee; the Editor of the *Gibraltar Chronicle*, Frances Cantos, was paid £150 for the use of facilities; and a stills photographer, Slim Simpson, received £150 for a photographic survey of the area of the shootings.

45 The role of Lieutenant-Colonel George Styles also calls for an early mention. A former head of bomb disposal in Northern Ireland, where he had earned the George Cross for conspicuous bravery, Colonel Styles had retired from the Army in 1974. Since then he had been in business as a security consultant specializing in explosives, weapons and ballistics. On being approached by THIS WEEK, Styles had agreed to act as a paid consultant and flew to Gibraltar, at the team's invitation, on 25 March. He visited the sites of the shootings, the location where it was thought the IRA had planned to explode their bomb, and talked personally to a number of eyewitnesses who had been

identified by the team. He was present when the interview with Carmen Proetta was filmed, and was able to see for himself how much she could have observed from the window of her flat overlooking the Shell filling station where two of the terrorists had been shot. Later he was able to use his professional knowledge in advising the THIS WEEK team on probable details of the shootings and in suggesting explanations for puzzling or conflicting aspects of the evidence. While in no sense a representative of the Ministry of Defence or the Security Services, and acting throughout in a private capacity, Colonel Styles nonetheless contributed an independent expertise both in private discussion and on film which gave greater depth and authority to the team's investigations than would otherwise have been available to them. The fact that some of Styles' opinions were later challenged by the Ministry of Defence served to underline his independent status.

46 These then were the principal actors in the making of 'Death on the Rock'. The programme team consisted of Roger Bolton (editor of THIS WEEK), Christopher Oxley (producer) and Julian Manyon (reporter), and the researchers, Alison Cahn and Eamon Hardy, the latter being transferred to another THIS WEEK project on 29 March. They were answerable to, and closely in touch with, Barrie Sales, Director of News and Current Affairs at Thames, and ultimately the Board of Thames Television. Filmed interviews were recorded in Gibraltar with Stephen Bullock, Josie Celecia, Carmen Proetta and Diana Treacy. Kenneth Asquez, who claimed to have been an eyewitness to the killing of the third IRA terrorist, was mentioned to Alison Cahn by a Gibraltarian, Major Randall, but he did not agree to be filmed, or named, or indeed to meet any of the team. He was seen on their behalf by a local lawyer, Christopher Finch, to whom he gave a statement that he later retracted. Colonel Styles acted as an expert consultant and made an informed and articulate contribution when filmed for the programme. In Spain, Manyon obtained an interview with a senior official at the Ministry of the Interior in Madrid, while Oxley and

the unit filmed a reconstruction of surveillance with the co-operation of the Spanish police in Malaga. Very little of the filming in Belfast of the IRA funeral was used, and none of the interview recorded with Gerry Adams. A sequence was included, however, showing the plight of a survivor of the IRA bombing incident at Enniskillen. Finally the programme contained an interview with a well-known barrister, George Carman QC, filmed in London, in which he stated the need for the Armed Forces to act within the rule of law and expressed the opinion that an inquiry by a High Court judge might be a more appropriate way than an inquest of investigating some of the matters surrounding the killings.

47 A verbatim transcript of the words spoken by the commentator and those interviewed in 'Death on the Rock' follows in the next chapter. Although an indication is given of the visuals, it is unavoidable that the written word can convey no more than a partial impression of a television programme.

Chapter Four

'Death on the Rock': the transcript

Picture	*Sound*
Pre-title Sequence	
Carmen Proetta (on camera):	There was no exchange of words on either side, no warning, nothing said; no screams, nothing; just the shots.
Stephen Bullock (on camera):	I should say they were from a distance of about four feet and that the firing was continuous; in other words, probably as fast as it's possible to fire.
THIS WEEK title sequence,	
Leading on to montage comprising: – general shots of the Rock – photo-montage of the three terrorists – excerpt from the reconstruction of the surveillance by Spanish police – Major Randall's video: shots of the three bodies being loaded on to an ambulance	Title music, Karelia Suite.

Opening Link

Jonathan Dimbleby (on camera and in studio):	Good evening.
Caption: *JONATHAN DIMBLEBY*	The killing by the SAS of three IRA terrorists in Gibraltar has provoked intense debate not only in Britain but throughout the world – and especially in the Republic of Ireland and the United States.
	There are perhaps those who wonder what the fuss is about, who ask: 'Does it really matter when or how they were killed?'; who say: 'They were terrorists; there's a war on; and we got to them before they got us.'
	However in the eyes of the law and of the state it is not so simple. The question, which goes to heart of the issue, is this: did the SAS men have the law on their side when they shot dead . . .
Photo-montage of the three terrorists	. . . Danny McCann, Sean Savage and Mairead Farrell who were unarmed at the time?
Photograph: ambulance and bodies at the petrol station	Were the soldiers acting in self-defence or were they operating what has become known as a 'shoot-to-kill policy' – simply eliminating a group of known terrorists outside the due process of law, without arrest, trial or verdict?

Jonathan Dimbleby (on camera):

There have been many calls for a public inquiry to establish the facts, though the Government has insisted that the Coroner's inquiry in Gibraltar is an adequate forum at which to discover the truth.

In either case, we believe that the evidence which THIS WEEK has uncovered for tonight's special programme is of critical importance for those who wish to find out what really happened in Gibraltar last month. Julian Manyon reports.

Caption: *DEATH ON THE ROCK REPORTER JULIAN MANYON*

Julian Manyon (voice-over):

Aerial shots of the Costa del Sol, and white car driving along road

Sunday morning on the Costa del Sol and among the holidaymakers, three Irish terrorists were planning a blood-bath. A white car headed down the coast road driven by an IRA bomber.

Wide shots: Rock of Gibraltar

The destination was Gibraltar – still Britain's vital military outpost at the entrance to the Mediterranean.

Shot of Union flag in breeze

Library film: guard mounting ceremony, Gibraltar

The IRA have admitted that their plan involved explosives, and all evidence suggests that the target was a ceremony that is a symbol of

British tradition on the Rock and a major tourist attraction.

Every Tuesday morning in normal times, soldiers and a military band parade in front of the Governor-General's residence.

Soldiers gathered at assembly point (Ince's Yard) after ceremony

The ceremony ends round the corner in a side street a hundred yards away, and it was here, at this moment, that the IRA apparently planned to set off a massive car bomb. Instead, three bombers were shot down after carrying out the first stage of their plan: driving in an empty car to secure a parking space as close as possible to their intended victims.

Lt Col George Styles and Julian Manyon walking in Ince's Yard

In the same street where a hundred and forty pounds of high explosive would have detonated, I spoke to a former explosives expert with the British Army. Lieutenant Colonel George Styles was for three years commander of bomb disposal in Ulster. He says the bomb would have annihilated soldiers and spectators alike.

Lt Col George Styles (on camera):

Well, we're talking about it in seconds, but in milliseconds; the car would disintegrate, the shrapnel could go nowhere – it would ricochet off the walls of the building

Caption: *LT COL GEORGE STYLES GC* Former Senior Bomb Disposal Officer, Northern Ireland

opposite and the wall behind; but above all that, you've got a tremendous concentration of blast because of the buildings so close together and the smallness of the area and so forth. And in the middle of all that, you've got people.

Julian Manyon (off camera):

And what would have been the effect on these people? The band, principally, of the Royal Anglian Regiment?

Lt Col Styles:

They wouldn't survive. People are fragmentable. They can be torn apart, and they are torn apart, by the effects of a concentrated blast. And I think anybody in this area would not survive.

Julian Manyon (voice-over):

Library film: Enniskillen bombing

Enniskillen on November 8th last year showed what a far smaller bomb can do to a mass of people; in this case, civilians gathered together for Remembrance Sunday.

The forty-pound bomb had been placed inside a building, next to the route of the Remembrance Day parade. In the wave of blast and flying rubble, eleven people died and more than fifty were wounded.

Ronnie Hill in hospital

Some wounds heal. Others last long after the memory of the atrocity has begun to fade. Until the bomb, Ronnie Hill was the much loved headmaster of the local high school. Today his wife, Noreen, keeps watch as he lives on in a deep coma that may sadly prove irreversible.

The coma began during emergency surgery to save Mr Hill's life, after the blast had badly damaged his lungs.

Noreen Hill (voice-over): His mind hasn't started to work yet. I mean he can hear us, he can hear what we're saying; but he can't see the difference in day and night. He can feel; but he can't move at all. On his own, he can't move.

Julian Manyon (off camera): And you're obviously sustained by the hope that he will get better?

Noreen Hill (on camera): Oh yes, we've faith that he will get better. The Lord will start his brain working in his time. And we've got to wait until that time.

Caption: *NOREEN HILL*

Julian Manyon (voice-over): After Enniskillen, the Provisionals' political leadership expressed regret. But in fact, the IRA was already planning the Gibraltar outrage.

Library film: Enniskillen bombing

Shot of suburban house   And one of the Gibraltar terrorists talked about Enniskillen in a recorded conversation in a suburban house in Belfast.

Mairead Farrell (voice-over, with subtitles):	It's all a political act. Even what happened in Enniskillen is a political act, because it wouldn't have happened if Britain weren't in Ireland.
Julian Manyon (voice-over): Sequence of photographs of Mairead Farrell	The speaker was Mairead Farrell who claimed on tape that she was against civilian casualties because they didn't help the struggle. She had recently been released after serving . . .
Footage of hotel on fire	. . . more than ten years in prison for planting bombs in a Belfast hotel, an act she committed at the age of nineteen. In the same tape she said she was lucky the police didn't shoot her when they found her outside the hotel.
Mairead Farrell (voice-over with subtitles):	Nowadays they don't take prisoners. You know I was lucky; I was lucky.
Julian Manyon (voice-over): Photograph of Farrell in prison cell	In prison, Farrell led the women's dirty protest, smearing excrement on the walls of their cells.
Graphic of IRA-Command structure with inset photograph of Farrell	After her release, she re-entered the IRA's military structure in a special unit attached to the general headquarters staff.

Graphic: Special Terrorist Unit with inset photographs of Savage, McCann and Farrell	In the same team were Sean Savage, a committed terrorist known for his bomb-making skills, and Danny McCann, known to British Intelligence as one of the IRA's most dangerous killers, who chose to shoot his victims at point-blank range. Last year, McCann was photographed with a cross that he claimed British soldiers had delivered to his door in Belfast.
	These were the three terrorists who came back dead from Gibraltar.
Film of the funeral	It's now clear that their unit's mission was to strike a major blow to revive IRA morale. Instead, they were tracked and died in what seemed a stunning military success for British forces. But in the way of Northern Ireland, that success is already turning sour; soured by the violence of the following days, and by the questions that still surround the deaths in Gibraltar. Were the terrorists, as some have charged, executed?
Carmen Proetta (on camera): Caption: *EYE WITNESS*	They put their hands up when they saw these men with the guns in their hands, but they couldn't say anything – there was no interchange of words, there was just shots. And once they dropped down, one of the men – this man who still had the gun in his hand – carried on

shooting. He bent down and carried on shooting at their heads.

Stephen Bullock
(on camera):

Caption: *EYE WITNESS*

Well, it seems to me that if you can get that close to someone, if you can get within four feet of your target, is it really necessary to shoot them, or even if it is necessary to shoot them, is it necessary to shoot them to kill them?

Julian Manyon
(voice-over):

Aircraft landing at airport

Caption:
5th NOVEMBER
Malaga Airport

It was on November 5th last year, four months before the shooting, that the IRA operation in southern Spain got under way. Arriving at Malaga Airport, a member of their special headquarters unit.

Passengers at airport and passport control

The terrorist who mingled with the other passengers was Daniel McCann, the gunman from Belfast, carrying a false Irish passport in the name of Reilly. As he went through passport control, he appeared to slip through routinely. But in reality, Spanish security police were already watching for him.

General beach shots

It turned out that McCann's destination was Torremolinos. In fact, the first tip-off that helped to locate the Irish terrorists here on the Costa del Sol . . .

Julian Manyon (on sea front to camera):

Caption: *JULIAN MANYON*

. . . came from London. I'm told that the Spanish police had received a message from the British authorities warning them that an IRA group could be trying to operate on Spanish soil. The message included a list of names, together with descriptions and possible aliases.

Julian Manyon (voice-over):
Exterior: Ministry of the Interior, Madrid

At the Ministry of the Interior in Madrid, the decision was taken to help the British as part of an agreed European strategy against terrorism.

Luis Aranz (on camera):

Caption: *LUIS ARANZ* Senior Adviser, Ministry of the Interior

Between the EEC countries we share the same approach to democracy, to freedom and to terrorism. So although there is not an obligation, a strict obligation, it is quite clear – an understanding of what is the terrorist and how to fight against.

Julian Manyon (off camera):

So in a case like Gibraltar, for example, there would have been no question – there was no question – about whether you were going to help or not? You really were committed to do it?

Luis Aranz:

Well, I feel the answer was given by the facts.

Julian Manyon (off camera):

There was no question but that you were going to go ahead and do what the British asked?

Luis Aranz: We did.

Julian Manyon (voice-over): General shots: beach/ Costa del Sol

The Spanish Security Service agreed to track the terrorists wherever they went, and keep the British fully informed of their movements. They searched as the IRA unit moved from hotel to hotel, using false passports in various different names.

General shots of a room full of computers

Details of thousands of tourists were sifted by police computers which checked hotel registration cards against lists of known false documents and names. By mid-November, they had pinpointed three terrorists:

Photographs of McCann/ Savage/silhouette

Daniel McCann, Sean Savage and another woman terrorist whom police in both Britain and Spain still refuse to name. The fourth member of the IRA unit, she travelled under the false name of Mary Parkin.

General shots of tourists in cafés

According to the Spanish Security Police, their men, disguised as tourists, managed to eavesdrop on the IRA team and overheard them discussing a bomb attack, though the target was not yet clear.

Aircraft taking off Caption: *15th NOVEMBER*

On November 15th last year, McCann and Savage flew from Malaga to Madrid and then back to Dublin. They were allowed to leave by the Spanish authorities, apparently after consultation with London. It seems that both Governments believed they would be back.

Library film: Memorial service at the Cenotaph, Enniskillen

A week later, at the Cenotaph in Enniskillen, Mrs Thatcher laid a wreath in honour of the people who died.

Caption: *22nd NOVEMBER* Enniskillen

On the day of the bombing she had declared that there should be no hiding place anywhere in the world for the men who did it. Now, she must have had on her desk the details of how an IRA unit had been detected in Spain. The question is: how much did the British already know about the terrorists' plans?

Library film: photo-call – Trevi Group of Interior Ministers

One clear hint came on December 9th, three months before the shootings in Gibraltar, when Home Secretary Douglas Hurd met with the interior ministers of the other EEC countries in Copenhagen. He warned this meeting of what is known as the Trevi Group on Terrorism that the IRA might be preparing to attack British institutions on the Continent.

Caption: *9th DECEMBER* Copenhagen

Building work by the Guard Room, Main Street, Gibraltar

In Gibraltar, just the day before the Home Secretary's speech, an unusual event provides another clue. The area where the parade normally takes place was suddenly

Caption: *GIBRALTAR*

closed for a face-lift, just as it is
today.

Copy of the *Gibraltar Chronicle*, showing announcement (as per commentary)

The announcement that guard mounting was suddenly suspended so the guardhouse could be painted, was made just the day before in the *Gibraltar Chronicle*. Was this coincidence? Not according to George Styles who has long experience of counter-terrorism.

Lt Col Styles
(on camera):

I would like to say that it was part of our planning. We stopped the parade; therefore there was no target; therefore no bomb is going to come. It seizes the initiative for a time being from the enemy. Now let's turn the parade on again – when we are ready to contain a possible situation that will arise. And in a way it would confirm to us that we're right in the intelligence we've gathered from them that they are still intending to blow up that parade on that day, in that place.

Julian Manyon
(voice-over):

Graphic: Coastal map of Gibraltar and Costa del Sol

Whatever the truth of that, the fact that Gibraltar was the target was certainly confirmed by close co-operation with a special Spanish police unit based at the other end of the Costa del Sol in the town of Malaga.

General shots: Malaga and police HQ	It was from Malaga, I'm told, that a joint Anglo-Spanish team tracked the terrorists when they resumed their operation in February this year. At police headquarters, officers from Spain's crack anti-terrorist squad worked with security officials from Britain.
Luis Aranz (on camera):	They will give information to the Spanish police; it is the Spanish police just to follow people and just to make any action on Spanish soil.
Julian Manyon (off camera):	So the British would have had, if you like, a liaison role, but not – would not have actually been doing the following themselves?
Luis Aranz:	Yes, of course.
Julian Manyon (voice-over) Caption: *TUESDAY, 23rd FEBRUARY* Gibraltar	On Tuesday, February 23rd, British soldiers in Gibraltar paraded once again in front of their newly painted guardhouse.
Library film: guard mounting ceremony Caption: *TUESDAY, 1st MARCH*	Among the tourists was the fourth member of the IRA team: the so-called Mary Parkin, who had been tailed here from Spain. She was seen studying the parade in detail. The following Tuesday, March 1st, she was seen again, and it was then, five days before the shootings, that events began to move very fast.

General shots: Belfast roof-tops

Caption: *WEDNESDAY, 2nd MARCH*
Belfast

Belfast. Wednesday, March 2nd. And the IRA's special headquarters unit began to move into action; no doubt alerted by Mary Parkin who then disappeared. That afternoon, the first member of the team slipped out of Belfast to catch a plane in Dublin.

Graphic: Map of Western Europe showing route travelled by Sean Savage (as per commentary)

Our information is that Sean Savage, the bomb maker, flew from Dublin to Brussels, and then on to Barcelona, where he apparently entered Spain without being immediately detected. He flew down to Malaga early on the following morning.

Exterior: Ministry of Defence

Caption: *MINISTRY OF DEFENCE*
London

But what the IRA didn't know was that inside the Defence Ministry in London, the joint operation centre was already on alert and preparing to defeat the IRA attack on the Rock of Gibraltar.

Exterior: Hotel Al-Andalus, followed by shots of guests checking in

Caption: *THURSDAY, 3rd MARCH*
Torremolinos

Thursday, March 3rd. And the bomber, Sean Savage, checked into a hotel in Torremolinos. Like any normal guest, he handed over his passport, but then asked for it back again before the receptionist had remembered to copy out the details. Savage had tricked the system, and police have reprimanded the hotel for their failure to register a terrorist.

General shots: Army check-point on Ulster country road	But that afternoon on the Irish border, another member of the team ran into trouble. Daniel McCann was apparently stopped and questioned by British soldiers on his way to Dublin. The Ministry of Defence have declined to comment on this reported episode.
Caption: *THURSDAY, 3rd MARCH* Northern Ireland	
Red Ford Fiesta car driving through Torremolinos	Friday, March 4th. Two days before the shooting. Sean Savage hired a red Ford Fiesta, the first of the team's three cars. It did more than a thousand miles, and Spanish police believe that it may have been used to fetch the explosive which had somehow been smuggled into another part of Spain.
Caption: *FRIDAY, 4th MARCH* Torremolinos	
General shots: tourists in streets of Torremolinos	That evening, Daniel McCann, the killer from West Belfast, arrived in Torremolinos. It appears that he was under surveillance all the way from Ireland to Spain. He may even have led the Spanish police who were following him to his friend, Sean Savage.
Exterior: Hotel Escandinava	Saturday, March 5th. And the Hotel Escandinava was where McCann and Savage were now staying – just one day before the shooting.
Caption: *SATURDAY, 5th MARCH* Torremolinos	
Hotel-room interior	They had checked into this room late on Friday night, and from now

on they were under constant surveillance. But the Spanish had completely missed one member of the team.

General shots: Malaga and its police headquarters

Caption: *MALAGA*

Then at twelve noon on Saturday, I'm told that an urgent message from London arrived at police headquarters in Malaga.

Photo-montage: Farrell

It said there is another terrorist and her name is Mairead Farrell. On the basis of this British tip-off, the Spanish police began to hunt for her.

Exterior: Marbesol car hire

Caption: *SUNDAY, 6th MARCH* Marbella

Woman's hand signing car-hire form in name of Katherine Smith

Sunday morning, March 6th. A car-hire firm in Marbella, just five hours before the shootings. Mairead Farrell walked in and gave a cash deposit to hire a car in the false name of Katherine Smith.

White car being driven into underground car-park

A few minutes later, she drove the white Ford Fiesta into an underground car-park in the centre of Marbella.

She drove it down to the lower level which is deserted on a Sunday morning. Police are working on the theory that the red car containing

Woman locking white car	the explosives was already parked here, and that Mairead Farrell now transferred them to the white car which had been hired with a fresh passport in a new name.
Photograph: explosives	A hundred and forty pounds of explosives were found in the white Ford Fiesta in the car-park two days after the shootings.
Julian Manyon (on camera outside car-park):	I'm told that until then neither the Spanish nor British police had any idea they were here. On the final Sunday of the operation, it was this vital question of where the explosives were hidden that came to obsess security officials in both Spain and Gibraltar.
Julian Manyon (voice-over): Aerial shots along Costa del Sol	While Mairead Farrell and the bomb were apparently out of sight, McCann and Savage had set out from Torremolinos, watched by the police. They met up with Farrell in Marbella, and the IRA team then set out for Gibraltar in two separate cars, both under surveillance. Tailing them, plain-clothes officers of Spain's élite anti-terrorist squad.
Reconstruction of Spanish surveillance: cars and helicopter following white Renault 5 car	The first IRA car was a white Renault 5 driven by Sean Savage. Later, police reported the red Ford with Farrell and McCann. Each car was expertly tailed, with a system the

Caption:
RECONSTRUCTION

Spanish police demonstrated for us on the same road that the terrorists took that Sunday. Up to four police drivers follow each suspect, constantly interchanging in order to avoid suspicion.

I am told by the Spanish Security Police that a constant flow of information about the terrorists' movements was radioed directly to British officials in Gibraltar. A police helicopter made sure that the watchers made no mistake.

The tempting target, symbol for the IRA of British imperialism, had become a carefully prepared trap.

Centre break for commercials

Julian Manyon
(voice over):

La Linea and Gibraltar border

Caption: *SUNDAY, 6th MARCH*
Spain–Gibraltar border

Sunday, March 6th. And the three IRA bombers prepared to cross the border into Gibraltar. Under the eyes of the Spanish police, their two cars met up, and then Savage drove off in the white Renault, leaving the red Ford and the other two terrorists behind in Spain.

White Renault 5 driving through the border controls

Caption: *GIBRALTAR*

Just before 1 pm, Savage drove into the border check-point, and the Spanish police allowed him to pass through.

On the Gibraltar side, British security officials took over the surveillance and they too allowed Savage's car to drive through unhindered. Just why the British security men did not stop a car that only two hours later came under suspicion as a dangerous car bomb is one of the key questions in the Gibraltar affair.

White Renault 5 drives across airfield and through Gibraltar to car-park in Ince's Yard

And the biggest question, as the car crossed the airfield towards the town of Gibraltar, is how much was known about what the white Renault actually contained. According to the Spanish Security Police, they thought it was possible that the car contained a bomb; but they were also working on the theory that the explosives had already been delivered to Gibraltar by sea, and that the car was now going to pick them up. British officials have made no public comment on what they believed, but there is little doubt that the car could have been intercepted before it reached the town centre.

Instead, Savage drove on, apparently unaware that nearby,

British troops, including SAS men, were lying in wait.

Under surveillance, he drove into the street where the Tuesday parade ends, and parked his car beside the ancient city wall.

General shots at Gibraltar–Spain border

Back at the border at around 2:30 that afternoon, the other two members of the IRA team crossed into Gibraltar on foot; and again, they were allowed to enter unimpeded.

General shots: Gibraltar street

In a street near the parked car they met up with Savage.

View of car-park by Ince's Yard, panning on to parked white Renault 5

And then at around half-past three, they all left the area on foot, leaving the parked white Renault behind them, unattended. Sir Geoffrey Howe gave this account in the House of Commons.

Sir Geoffrey Howe (voice-over with sub-titles):

Their presence and actions near the parked Renault car gave rise to strong suspicion that it contained a bomb, which appeared to be corroborated by a rapid technical examination of the car.

Caption: *RT HON SIR GEOFFREY HOWE* Foreign Secretary

Photo-montage: House of Commons interior; Sir Geoffrey Howe (inset)

Julian Manyon
(voice-over):

Shots of white Renault 5 from different angles

In fact, the car was later found to contain no explosive device, and according to an expert, a rapid examination should have shown that there was no significant bomb in it.

Lt Col Styles on camera

George Styles ran bomb-disposal operations in Northern Ireland during his tour of duty there.

Lt Col Styles:

Caption: (as before)

Well, I'm sure that the army bomb-disposal man was somewhere near, and observing the scene, and when the white car came in he would be told that that's the terrorist bringing in the car, and I'm sure he would have quickly seen that it carried no significant weight of explosive.

Julian Manyon
(off camera):

How would he have seen that?

Lt Col Styles:

Well, the posture of the car on its springs is dictated . . .

Shot of back of white Renault 5 depressing when weight put in boot

. . . by the weight it's carrying, and if you put a hundredweight of cement in the boot of a car, which is about car-bomb size, it shows. Agreed, there could have been a smaller bomb inside it, and I expect the bomb-disposal man anticipated such. He would have probably said this hasn't got a significant bomb in it, but I'm going to treat it with care.

Julian Manyon
(voice-over):

Photograph of the white
Renault 5 used by the
terrorists (as per
commentary)

A photograph of the real car taken
that day appears to support that
view. It shows it riding high on its
springs, with no load over the wheel
arch.

General shots:
– Main Street (Gibraltar)

At around 3:30, the terrorists began
to walk back towards the border. It's
now believed that the next phase in
their plan would have been to bring
in the real car bomb. They would
then have put it in their parking
space in time for the parade on
Tuesday.

– Landport Ditch

– bullet-ridden petrol
pump

– the Shell petrol station

They left the old town and were
more than a mile from the parked
car when Farrell and McCann, a
hundred yards in front of Savage,
reached a petrol station which was
closed on Sunday. Then suddenly, a
burst of shots rang out . . .

Major Randall's video:
policeman by covered
bodies of Farrell and
McCann as ambulance
arrives

. . . and in less than a minute all
three terrorists were dead – shot by
the SAS. In the House of Commons
Sir Geoffrey Howe gave this
account of what happened.

Sir Geoffrey Howe
(voice-over):

On their way towards the border,
they were challenged by the security
forces. When challenged, they made
movements which led the military
personnel, operating in support of

the Gibraltar police, to conclude that their own lives and the lives of others were under threat. In the light of this response, they were shot. Those killed were subsequently found not to have been carrying arms.

Julian Manyon
(voice-over):
General shots panning across Laguna and Glacis Estates

Since that statement to the House of Commons, THIS WEEK has spoken to large numbers of residents in all the blocks of flats overlooking the area where the terrorists died. We have found no one who heard a challenge being made.

Photo-montage of witnesses:
rear view of anonymous woman (Diana Treacy); Josie Celecia; Stephen Bullock; Carmen Proetta

We have interviewed four key witnesses to the shootings. Their accounts raise serious questions about what really happened that afternoon; for they say that the British soldiers opened fire without warning, and none of them saw the IRA bombers make any threatening movements.

Photo-montage: George Jeger House (the Celecias' flat marked by a ring); photograph of Josie Celecia (inset)

The first witness is a housewife, Josie Celecia, whose flat is on the second floor opposite the petrol station.

Josie Celecia:

Josie Celecia looking out of window, followed by

Well, I saw these two couple, and I was staring at the man because he had spiky, blond, short hair, you know. Then all of a sudden, I took

shots of her view panning along Winston Churchill Avenue

my sight off them, and looked to the adventure playground.

Josie Celecia
(on camera):

Caption: *JOSIE CELECIA*
Eye witness

Suddenly, I heard two shots – there were about two shots. So I was just looking from where that came from. And all of a sudden I saw the woman, you know, the couple on the floor.

Julian Manyon
(voice-over):

Street-plan graphic: Josie Celecia's and Carmen Proetta's version of events

What Josie saw in the first seconds were the terrorists, but little of the SAS men who shot them.

But our second witness had a different view, with what seems to have been a more complete picture of the shooting.

The first thing she says she witnessed was a Gibraltar police car arrive from the direction of the border and suddenly screech to a halt on the other side of the road from the two IRA bombers.

Carmen Proetta at her window

Seen at her window, the witness is Carmen Proetta.

Carmen Proetta:

I looked out of the window . . .

View from Carmen Proetta's window,

. . . and all of a sudden I saw a car – police car. It stops all of a sudden,

followed by Carmen Proetta on camera	and the doors were open, all of them, the four of them, and three men came out dressed in jeans and jackets, jumped over the intersection barrier in the road, guns in hand . . .
Caption: *CARMEN PROETTA* Eye witness	
Julian Manyon (voice-over):	Carmen Proetta has given us a sworn affidavit detailing what she saw. She says she is willing to testify at the inquest, though she has not yet been approached by the police.
Graphic: Carmen Proetta's affidavit (with inset photograph of Carmen Proetta)	
Street-plan graphic (as per commentary)	In a statement that will cause great controversy, she says that the first two terrorists had their hands in the air at the moment they were shot by the SAS. She also says that the British soldiers fired the first shot without warning as they jumped over the central barrier in the middle of the road.
Carmen Proetta (on camera):	They didn't do anything, they just jumped with their guns in their hands, and they just went and shot these people. That's all. They did not say anything, they didn't scream, they didn't shout, they didn't do anything. These people were turning their heads back to see what was happening, and when they saw these men had the guns in their

hands they just put their hands up. It looked like the man was protecting the girl, because he stood in front of her, but there was no chance. I mean they went to the floor immediately; they dropped.

Julian Manyon (voice-over):

Stephen and Mrs Bullock walking along Smith Dorrien Avenue with baby son in push-chair, followed by shot of Stephen Bullock's view of petrol station

At the same moment, Stephen Bullock, a British lawyer, was walking with his wife and baby son. He heard shots and looked towards the petrol station.

Stephen Bullock (on camera):

Caption: *STEPHEN BULLOCH* (sic) Eye witness

(hand gesture off camera)

(raises hands on either side of his head, palms facing camera)

Outside the petrol station I saw a man who I'm fairly sure was wearing a bright yellow short-sleeved shirt, standing with both hands outstretched holding a gun, like this, and firing very rapidly into another man with blond hair, wearing a white shirt, who was falling backwards with his hands like this. And falling back almost in slow motion. He went right down and the firing continued. He was still being shot at as he went down.

Julian Manyon (off camera):

And the moment these shots were being fired into him, how close were the two men together?

Stephen Bullock: About as far as I am from you; say, four feet.

Julian Manyon
(off camera):   Really close range?

Stephen Bullock: Oh yes, yes. Undoubtedly. I mean close enough; let's put it this way, I think with one step he could have actually touched the person he was shooting.

Julian Manyon
(voice-over):   Looking from her window, Josie Celecia saw the terrorists on the ground and an SAS man still pointing his pistol at them.

Josie Celecia seen looking from her window

Julian Manyon
(off camera):   As you saw the two lying on the ground, and another man standing above them, what happened?

Josie Celecia
(on camera):   I heard shots, about four or five shots.

Julian Manyon
(off camera):   More shots?

Josie Celecia: Si.

Julian Manyon
(off camera):   What were they like?

Josie Celecia: Continuously.

Douglas Celecia (off camera):	Automatic fire . . . no? automatic . . . bla-bla-bla-bla . . .
Josie Celecia:	Like that . . . One after the other.
Julian Manyon (voice-over): Carmen Proetta at her window	Carmen Proetta also saw a gunman fire at the two people who were lying on the ground.
Carmen Proetta (on camera):	Yes, he bent down and with the two hands – he got his gun like that and went on shooting at them.
Julian Manyon (off camera):	How many times do you think he shot?
Carmen Proetta:	Two times at least.
Julian Manyon (voice-over): Photo-montage: Shell petrol station; Farrell and McCann (inset)	Mairead Farrell and Daniel McCann were the two terrorists who died by the petrol station. According to our information, which has not been officially confirmed, Farrell was shot twice in the face and once under the left breast, in the area of the heart. McCann, the most dangerous terrorist, was shot eight or nine times, several times in the chest and once below the chin – the bullet exiting through the top of his head.
Photograph of Savage	Sean Savage, the third terrorist, was not killed in the first burst of shots . . .

Overhead shot of petrol station then panning down to Landport Ditch	. . . as he was about a hundred yards behind the others. For some reason, perhaps because he saw or heard the shooting, he ran back towards the old town, pursued by at least one SAS man.
View of tree in Landport Ditch	Savage died round a corner beside a large oak tree.
Graphic: Position of fourth witness (Diana Treacy) in relating to Savage and gunman	According to our fourth witness, she was near the tree when a man later identified as Savage ran past her. He was pursued by a second man who had a gun in his left hand.
Unidentified woman eyewitness: (Diana Treacy speaking back to camera) Caption: *EYE WITNESS*	He just lifted his left arm and I heard the first shot. It was then when I looked back and saw the other man that was running fall back as the other man continued shooting at him.
Julian Manyon (on camera):	Did you hear any warning of any kind given by the man with the gun?
Eyewitness:	No, no.
Julian Manyon (on camera):	Did you hear him say: 'Stop, police'?
Eyewitness:	No, no. Just happened so sudden.
Julian Manyon (on camera):	He just opened fire, just like that?
Eyewitness:	Yes.

Julian Manyon
(voice-over):

Major Randall's video:
policeman standing near
Savage's covered body in
Landport Ditch

Our witness says she was only a few
feet from the soldier when he
opened fire. Later, Savage was
found lying face upwards beside the
tree. The witness insists that he was
shot in the back, with more shots
fired as he lay on the ground.

Eyewitness:
(Diana Treacy back to
camera)

I looked back and I saw the other
man that was running just being
shot, and just fall back.

Julian Manyon
(on camera):

Fall backwards?

Eyewitness:

And he was bouncing on the floor
when the other man continued
shooting at him about three or four
shots more. And I thought he was
dead.

Julian Manyon
(on camera):

You mean you saw the man who was
shot, was shot in the back?

Eyewitness:

Yes, through the back.

Julian Manyon
(voice over):

Graphic: position of
Asquez's car

At this point the female witness ran
away, but we have obtained a
dramatic account of what allegedly
happened next from another witness
who was in a car only a few yards
back. Also wishing to protect his
identity, he has given a detailed
statement to a lawyer representing
THIS WEEK.

Male voice-over
(with subtitles):

The man on the ground was lying on his back. The man standing over this man had his foot on the man's chest. I could see that he also had a gun in his hand . . . I then saw the gunman point his gun deliberately at the man that was lying on the floor and fire two or three times into him at point-blank range. I was horrified by what I saw . . .

Julian Manyon
(voice-over):

Major Randall's video: shot of ground with chalk outline of Savage's body, and blood stains around area of neck

Our information is that the bullets that killed Savage were fired into his neck. Only the pathologist's report at the inquest can establish what range they were fired from.

Major Randall's video: shots of ambulance at petrol station

A vital question is why the terrorists were not arrested. Was minimum force used? The 'yellow card' rules in Northern Ireland say a soldier may only fire at a person who is likely to endanger life, and there is no other way to prevent the danger. For a fuller legal definition we asked George Carman, a leading QC.

George Carman QC
(on camera):

Caption: *GEORGE CARMAN QC*

The general rule of law is fairly simple to state: such force as is reasonable, or reasonably necessary to prevent crime, in order to defend yourself or to defend others, is justified in law. But quite obviously, having stated the general principle, everything turns on the particular facts of the case. At the one extreme there is no unfettered licence to kill; at the other extreme, extreme danger requires extreme measures to be taken.

Julian Manyon
(voice-over):

Rear shot of white Renault 5 followed by overhead view of Ince's Yard car-park

The Renault car in the centre of town was the basis of fears that there was extreme danger to the public. It was suspected that the car contained a bomb.

Graphic: newspaper titles and cuttings

In the week following the shooting, several newspapers carried stories, based on Whitehall briefings, suggesting that the terrorists could have suddenly set off a car bomb by radio using a miniature device concealed in pocket or handbag.

General panoramic shots of Gibraltar

Not mentioned was the fact that the car was almost a mile and a half from the point where the terrorists died, with buildings and a city wall in between.

Julian Manyon and Lt Col Styles walking up to and through Landport Tunnel

We asked George Styles if a remote-control explosion had been a possibility.

Lt Col Styles:

Caption (as before)

Well, I would say very unlikely indeed. There's so much building work, and the undulations of the ground and so on . . .

Lt Col Styles on camera	. . . I doubt if they could ever set that car – the white car – off from the other side of the tunnel. You know, on the Rock, there's all sorts of radio waves going about; if they could send a signal, I think it would be swamped anyway by the other communications.
Julian Manyon (voice-over): Exterior shots: Ministry of Defence	Last week, we asked the Ministry of Defence in London if the IRA has ever set off a radio-controlled bomb at a range of more than a mile out of line of sight. The Ministry declined to comment, giving the forthcoming inquest as their reason.
Library film: soldiers in Gibraltar streets	Another strange fact is that according to the Gibraltar police who were involved, the area of the Renault car was only cleared at 4 pm – after the three terrorists had been killed, and at least two hours after the car was parked. It will no doubt be argued at the inquest that these facts leave out the uncertainties, confusion and fears that often dog military operations. And under the law, the soldiers involved will only have to demonstrate that they held a reasonable belief that the terrorists represented an extreme danger.

Photo-montage of the three terrorists	And it could be argued that a threat to life was posed by the nature of the terrorists themselves. All three had violent records, and McCann was known to be a deadly killer. There was a possibility that he or the others was carrying a concealed weapon, and their reactions, if challenged, could not be predicted.
Photograph of Sir Geoffrey Howe Caption: as per quote in commentary	Sir Geoffrey Howe told the House of Commons that, when challenged, the terrorists made movements 'which led the soldiers to conclude that their lives, and the lives of others, were under threat'.
Carmen Proetta at her window View of petrol station from Mrs Proetta's window	But in her most controversial statement, witness Carmen Proetta, who saw the deaths of Farrell and McCann by the petrol station, says that the incident began with the sound of a police siren, and that there were no threatening movements from the terrorists.
Carmen Proetta (on camera): Caption (as before)	No. There was no sharp movement. It was the movement of a person that is walking towards somewhere, doesn't know what's going on when they hear a siren, and it's a normal gesture of somebody that just moves when they hear somebody or some noise, or some sort of unfamiliar or whatever noise.

Julian Manyon
(off camera):

And then, as they turned, they must have seen coming towards them over this railing men with guns. What movements did they make then – these two terrorists?

Carmen Proetta:

They didn't make any movements – they put their hands up. I believe I've said it before. Yes, they just put their hands up . . .

Julian Manyon
(off camera):

Was this a reflexive gesture, or were they actually trying to give themselves up, do you think?

Carmen Proetta:

It was like giving themselves up, like – unresisting gesture.

Julian Manyon
(off camera):

An unresisting gesture?

Carmen Proetta:

An unresisting . . . yes.

Julian Manyon
(off camera):

As if they were trying to surrender, is what you're saying?

Carmen Proetta:

Yes, like saying 'what's happening? We haven't done anything,' or some sort of like that.

Julian Manyon and Lt Col
Styles at petrol station

Lt Col Styles
(gesticulating on camera):

Well this is the killing ground . . .
(fade out)

Julian Manyon
(voice-over):

George Styles, who is also a ballistics expert, believes that what Carmen saw could be explained by the impact of bullets travelling faster than the speed of sound, striking the terrorists, and throwing their hands in the air. But reviewing the shooting as a whole, he believes that a clear-cut decision was taken: to eliminate the terrorists as cleanly and safely as possible.

Lt Col Styles
(on camera):

Caption (as before)

I look at the whole piece as being two active service units waging war, and thank goodness our side won. The battlefield was one of their choosing in the first place – that is, the general community – and I think it would be reckless for the security forces to have tangled with these people, who may well have been armed, as we've seen on other occasions; so taking them out quickly, cleanly and without other people getting hurt – that seems to be the only way.

George Carman QC
(on camera):

Caption (as before)

What is important on the one hand is that Her Majesty's Government take all proper, effective steps to stamp out the scourge of terrorism, and I imagine that's beyond dispute. Equally, on the other hand, it is important that the measures that are taken, however extreme and necessary they are, fall within the rule of law, which governs us all; because even the activities of soldiers or police officers who have to face the awful problem of terrorism has to be conducted within the framework of the rule of law. So, of course, it is desirable that there should be a full examination of what actually occurred.

Julian Manyon
(voice-over):

Photograph of petrol station

Caption: 'No independent witness has told us they saw or heard a challenge'

Our inquiries into the shootings in Gibraltar have revealed a number of important and troubling issues. No independent witness has told us that they saw or heard the security forces challenge the terrorists.

Photograph: Carmen Proetta

Caption: 'Two terrorists shot with their hands in the air'

Carmen Proetta has sworn in an affidavit that she saw two of the bombers shot with their hands in the air.

Photograph of Diana Treacy
(from behind):
Caption: 'Terrorist shot in the back as he ran away'

Another witness says she saw the third terrorist shot in the back as he ran away.

Photo-montage: Carmen Proetta and silhouette of anonymous male figure

Caption: 'The terrorists being finished off on the ground'

Two witnesses say that they saw the terrorists being finished off while they lay on the ground. And deeply disturbing . . .

Photograph: Lt Col Styles, followed by Photograph: white Renault 5	George Styles, an acknowledged expert on bomb disposal, says that the security forces should have known within minutes of examining the white Renault 5 that there was no significant bomb in the car.
Caption: 'The security forces should have known . . . that there was no significant bomb in the car'	

Major Randall's video:
– ambulance driving away from petrol station

Clearly, all these questions require deep and complex investigation to establish the truth. But doubt remains as to whether that will happen.

– Savage's body being loaded on to ambulance . . . ambulance moving off . . .

One reason for disquiet is the role in the shootings of the Gibraltar police. They apparently drove the SAS men to the scene, and certainly took them away again minutes later. One question is whether the police force that helped to carry out the operation is the right body to investigate it.

General shots: The Supreme Court building, Gibraltar

Another question concerns the nature of the Coroner's court where this highly controversial inquest will eventually take place in this small outpost of Empire.

General shots: Felix Pizzarello leaving the Supreme Court building and walking along Main Street

The court can produce a wide range of verdicts, including, in theory, homicide, but Mr Felix Pizzarello, the Coroner, would be the first to admit that both his experience and

powers to investigate are limited.
The Prime Minister has declared
that his inquest is where the facts
should be established; but a leading
QC has doubts.

George Carman QC
(on camera):

Caption (as before)

The Coroner's court is a perfectly
proper place to investigate ordinary
fatalities. But where great public
interest and matters of public
importance are involved, such as
this case that you've been talking
about, it seems to me desirable that
some senior judicial power, such as
a High Court judge, would be much
more appropriately appointed to
investigate a matter – and preside
over an inquiry of this kind.

Julian Manyon
(off camera):

Do you believe this case is so
important that the Government
should actually consider such
extraordinary steps in order to
clarify the facts?

George Carman QC:

It's not for me to advise Her
Majesty's Government as to what
steps they should take. But clearly,
from everything you say, the
programme indicates that there are
serious important public issues
involved and, speaking as a lawyer,
one is always anxious that where
there is contest on the facts in such
important areas, they should be
properly and efficiently investigated.

Closing link

Jonathan Dimbleby
(on camera and in studio):

That report by Julian Manyon was made, as you may have detected, without the co-operation of the British Government which says that it will make no comment until the inquest.

As our film contained much new evidence hitherto unavailable to the Coroner, we are sending the transcripts to his court in Gibraltar, where it's been made clear to us that all such evidence is welcomed.

From THIS WEEK, good night.

Closing title sequence and credits

Title music, Karelia Suite.

END

Chapter Five

Cleared for transmission

48 The criticisms made of the preparation and presentation of 'Death on the Rock', and of the decision to broadcast it, depend in large part on what its true meaning and effect are perceived to have been. Opinions on this question differed widely, and continue to do so. On the one hand, critics of the programme have consistently maintained that it plainly implied that the terrorists were murdered. It is claimed that a single question was posed, namely whether the terrorists had been executed, and answered in the affirmative. The programme's defenders, on the other hand, are adamant that the true effect of the programme was merely to lay before the viewing public certain evidence and to suggest that the evidence gave rise to important and disturbing questions calling for careful examination by an authoritative tribunal such as a judicial inquiry.

49 Such polarity of opinion has not been confined to the interested parties. For example, a review by Geoffrey Levy in the *Daily Mail* on 29 April 1988 stated, in forceful terms, that the programme was 'woefully one-sided', and had presented its makers' belief that the terrorists had been murdered 'with the summary justice of an execution without trial'. Conversely, William Holmes, writing in *The Times* on the same day, felt that the programme was 'a significant, thoroughly responsible and serious examination of a most disturbing case', and that it was in no sense a 'trial by television', but on the contrary 'simply raised questions and suggested that they required deep examination'. These two review articles are reprinted, with permission, at the end of this chapter.

50 We believe that the true effect of the programme lies somewhere between these two extremes. There is no reason to doubt that

the interpretation which attributed to the programme the characteristics of a trial at which the soldiers had been found guilty without being heard was genuinely felt and honestly expressed. We can understand the feelings of those who saw in the programme an unfair indictment of servants of the Crown carrying out a highly dangerous mission. We accept that the tendency of the evidence presented was to suggest a possibility that the terrorists had been unlawfully killed, perhaps murdered. Nor were alternative explanations canvassed in any depth. Yet these considerations do not lead us to believe that the programme concluded that the terrorists had been unlawfully killed. The true interpretation, it seems to us, is that the programme pointed towards one possible explanation. By 'possible' we do not mean mere speculation or conjecture, but a real possibility suggested by credible evidence and requiring proper examination.

51 To the extent that the programme was mainly devoted to one possible explanation, it could be regarded as 'one-sided'. But there is a difference between a programme whose lack of balance is apparent to the viewer, and is explicitly drawn to his attention (so-called personal view programmes are one example), and one which, while giving an appearance of impartiality, contrives to lead the viewer to a particular conclusion. This may result from the selection of evidence, or the suppression of explanations within the knowledge of the programme-maker, but inconsistent with the conclusion. 'Death on the Rock' made it clear enough that no official account of the shootings was available beyond what the Foreign Secretary had said in the House of Commons on 7 March. Viewers should not have been in any doubt that the material in the programme had been obtained without the assistance of the authorities.

52 Investigative programmes which deal with controversial issues are sometimes condemned as 'trial by television'. 'Death on the Rock' was so described (chapter One, paragraph 4). We therefore think it is necessary to explain the distinction between the

methodology of television programmes and trials. A contested trial involves the deployment of competing versions of the facts which are then subjected to testing by adversarial process and culminates in a firm conclusion by an independent tribunal as to which version of the facts is to be preferred. The nature of an investigative television programme is quite different. It presents chosen subjects to the audience focusing attention on certain issues. The process is journalistic – intuitive and assertive – rather than forensic, and its principal elements are the information uncovered by the programme-makers and their own assessment of its implications. It will often be the case that the information is incomplete, if only because certain interested parties may not be willing to co-operate. Nor can such information as is available be subjected to the rigorous examination which is the feature of a trial. These considerations underpin the requirements of impartiality in the *Television Programme Guidelines*, and the specific reference to the need to avoid an investigation turning into a case for the prosecution or defence. How did 'Death on the Rock' accord with these precepts?

53 In answering this question we have found it instructive to compare that part of the programme which dealt with the surveillance issue (pages 36–48 of the transcript in chapter Four) with that part which dealt with the shootings. In reporting the surveillance of the terrorists by the Spanish police up to the Gibraltar frontier the commentary made several factual assertions – where, when, how and by whom the surveillance was carried out. The overall effect was to suggest to the viewer that he was being told exactly what had happened. The fact that the accuracy of this reconstruction was later challenged by the Foreign and Commonwealth Office does not impinge upon this observation; we consider it in a different context in the next chapter.

54 By contrast, the coverage of the shootings left events which were potentially controversial to be described by the eyewitnesses as they believed they had happened. The commentary largely confined itself to reporting or summarizing the evidence of the

eye-witnesses and to posing certain questions which arose from their evidence. In eight instances the commentary reported details of the shootings as fact (see chapter Four, pages 50, 57, 58 and 59), but in none of these instances were the details controversial. In each case where the evidence of a witness was perceived to be controversial, it was clear from the context that what was reported was what the witness was saying he or she had seen.

55 This analysis of the *content* of the programme leads us to the opinion that the format and conclusion of 'Death on the Rock' did not offend against the due impartiality requirements of the IBA and the Broadcasting Act. We are in agreement with the IBA that taken as a whole the programme was acceptable. The question of the possible *effect* of the programme in terms of prejudicing the inquest and contaminating the evidence is considered separately later in this report.

56 We have asked the IBA about the amount of time that is needed for the proper exercise of the Authority's regulatory functions in a situation of this kind. Lord Thomson told us that he was constantly striving for more time in which to make decisions on those occasions, relatively few in number, when a programme needs to be viewed by the Chairman of the IBA personally before a decision is taken on its transmission. In the case of 'Death on the Rock', however, he insisted that even if there had been more notice he would have reached the same decision. Indeed in a notably frank public comment Lord Thomson admitted that it was paradoxical in the light of the controversy which followed, unsurpassed in his experience in the intensity of the passions aroused, that the decision to allow the screening of 'Death on the Rock' had not seemed a difficult one at the time. He went on:

'My colleagues and I saw no reason why the IBA should prevent Thames's journalists interviewing those who claimed to be eyewitnesses and investigating the affair exactly as numerous other journalists have done ever since the shootings, provided the criminal record of the terrorists and the enormity of the outrage they planned was made clear and the legal position had been established to our satisfaction.' (*Daily Telegraph* 28 December 1988)

57 The grounds for rejecting the Foreign Secretary's request that the programme be postponed are considered in some detail in chapter Eleven. Here we are simply concerned to draw attention to the relationship between time and the quality of decision-making. Inevitably time will be short. Production schedules are always tight, caused partly by the technical processes, partly by the number of people involved, sometimes in current affairs television by developing events, and always by the desire for perfection. 'Death on the Rock' had a longer than average period of gestation of approximately seven weeks. At least since 11 April, on which date the IBA's Director of Television was present when the specially extended running time was agreed by the Network Programme Controllers (see chapter Three, paragraph 39), the exceptional interest the programme was likely to attract, and was intended to attract, was known to the IBA. The *TV Times* listing, for example, claimed that the special edition of THIS WEEK would come up 'with startling new evidence which challenges previously accepted views'. On 21 April Bolton offered the IBA a preview which was tentatively arranged at Thames for the following Monday, 25 April. He said that the programme could then be viewed complete except for the commentary and some graphics. A guide script would be available. The provisional arrangement was to be confirmed on the day. But when Monday came he was informed that the IBA staff preferred to see the programme complete at its own headquarters in Brompton Road. Bolton replied that he would try and get the material sent round to the Authority by the following evening. At about 6:00 pm on Tuesday, 26 April, two days before transmission, a copy of the script was dispatched, with a cassette of the undubbed programme following later in the evening. The dubbing of the commentary did not begin until the Wednesday and was completed on the day of transmission,

Thursday, 28 April. We are told by THIS WEEK that this is the normal practice.

58 The preview of 'Death on the Rock' finally took place at Brompton Road on Wednesday, 27 April. The programme was still incomplete in the sense that the sound had not yet been recorded and married up to the picture. Two days before, on the Monday, the earlier version had been viewed by Thames' Director of News and Current Affairs, Barrie Sales. Some changes were made to the commentary at this stage. The IBA also asked for three alterations to be made to the script for the commentary. Senior staff in the Programme Division, accompanied by the IBA's Officer for Northern Ireland, felt that the reporter's summing-up suggested too strongly that the Coroner's inquest would be unable to establish the truth, and that the Gibraltar police evidence would be unreliable. These two points were readily accepted. On the third point, the Editor of THIS WEEK came back to justify a phrase that had been queried about the Prime Minister's prior knowledge of the detection of an IRA unit in Spain. His argument was accepted, and this statement (see chapter Four, page 39) was not amongst those subsequently challenged by the Foreign Office in their evidence to our Inquiry. At this stage IBA staff also spoke to a Thames lawyer to check the legal position, particularly in relation to the question of possible contempt of court. They received satisfactory assurances. The IBA officials were content with the final version of the script and reported accordingly to an escalating hierarchy of Director of Television, Director-General, and finally Chairman, each of whom viewed the programme throughout the evening or later that night. Despite all this activity, the fact remains that when the Foreign Secretary first spoke to Lord Thomson on the evening of Tuesday, 26 April no-one on the IBA staff had yet seen the programme, albeit in its unfinished state.

59 We pressed the IBA about this timetable, but were assured it was nothing out of the ordinary. We were told it was not the practice to preview partly-completed programmes. The IBA

seeks to avoid getting drawn into the editorial process, its responsibility being 'to see whether a programme as offered for transmission meets the requirements both of the IBA and of the Statutes'. We were informed that the IBA has, on a number of occasions, stopped programmes on Northern Ireland on the day of transmission. It was contended that it would be neither justified nor fair to suggest that the Authority had left itself insufficient time to exercise its regulatory functions. The Authority's reply also commented that Thames was 'late in producing the final version of the film even though they knew the time scale to which the IBA wished to work'.

60 In setting out at some length the details of the tortuous process of clearing a programme for transmission on Independent Television we seek to illustrate where responsibility lies and how it is exercised. The programme company is primarily responsible for the journalism, but it does not relinquish an interest in the decision to screen its programme. The IBA regards itself as primarily responsible for the decision to transmit. As we have seen, that distinction does not, and should not, preclude the IBA from asking for such editorial changes as it may consider necessary in order to ensure that a programme meets its requirements.

61 We do not question the decision that 'Death on the Rock' was acceptable for transmission and do not therefore suggest that in this instance the timetable allowed inadequate time for consultation with the programme-makers and internal discussion. We do, however, stress the need for flexibility in the regulatory procedures. The production cycle of a regular weekly current affairs programme makes it inappropriate to lay down rules about the degree of completeness required before material is viewed and where such previews should take place. What is paramount is to devise and keep in good repair working practices which are capable of securing the confidence of the programme-makers, while at the same time having the capacity to respond to unexpected situations.

Review by Geoffrey Levy published in the *Daily Mail* on 29 April 1988.

'A WOEFULLY ONE-SIDED LOOK AT THE KILLINGS'
'THERE is fact and there is speculation.

'Any reasonable viewer watching This Week would have been left in no doubt that the personal wishes and orders of Mrs Thatcher were carried out to the letter when three IRA bombers were shot dead by the SAS in Gibraltar.

'Unimaginable, maybe, but that was the message. The telling phrase, the killing phrase, was "must have". She "*must have* had on her desk the details of how an IRA unit had been detected in Spain."

Accusing
'Now I have no idea how closely Mrs Thatcher or any other Prime Minister is involved in the sharp end of individual anti-IRA actions. Not much, I should think. But the accusing phrase was slipped in like a stiletto after a highly emotional and dramatic post-Enniskillen build-up in which her Cenotaph words – that there must be "no hiding place anywhere in the world for the men who did it" – were repeated.

'And from that moment, as we saw reporter Julian Manyon's version of how the bombers were traced through Spanish police computers checking immigration cards and tracked until they crossed the border like Big Game, no viewer could possibly have shed the astonishing mental implant that nothing was happening, or was going to happen, that was not under the direct control of Mrs Thatcher.

'Of course "*must have*" is one of those handy phrases journalists use when they are short of facts, let alone proof. It is a speculative probe, never to be used as here, carelessly. And it was typical of this woefully one-sided look at the killings on the Rock.

'George Styles, the George Medal-winning bomb disposal figure, was the sole expert, unchallenged and unopposed by an alternative view. He was gracious enough to suggest caution in one or two of the pronouncements, but these were glossed over with unsavoury speed as though they were insignificant asides.

'His explanation that there could not have been the suspected 140 lb of high explosives in the bombers' hired car was clear enough – it was not weighed down low on its springs. That a smaller bomb was possible was uttered in indecent haste and not exposed to further examination.

'Another aside concerned the pivotal moment in the programme:

When the pretty face of 42-year-old translator Carmen Proetta, looking from the window where she saw the slayings, insisted that two of the gang put their hands up in a non-threatening gesture of surrender.

'Styles's alternative suggestion to the cold-blooded killing he believed it was – that their arms could have jerked up from the impact of being hit by bullets – was pushed through the script with, I thought, wantonly indecent haste.

'Nor was there a single alternative ballistics and military view presented to that of George Styles, chatting away in the sunshine, that he would have thought the decision taken was to eliminate the gang as efficiently as possible.

'This Week plainly thought there was no need. They knew what they believed. They presented it with the summary justice of an execution without trial – the very thing the reporter with his dramatically throbbing voice must have believed he was exposing to the world.

'Yes, he *must have*.'

Review by William Holmes published in *The Times* on 29 April 1988.

'QUESTION OF TRUTH'

'Last night Thames Television went ahead with its planned showing of a *This Week Special* called "Death on the Rock", a report on the shooting of three IRA bombers in Gibraltar, in spite of requests from Sir Geoffrey Howe to the IBA that the programme should be postponed.

'From where I sit, out of the political firing line, the report seemed a significant, thoroughly responsible and serious examination of a most disturbing case. To suppress the programme would have been far more "irresponsible" (the Foreign Office's word) than the decision to show it, if the establishment of truth is to be the final criterion. Julian Manyon's script jumped to no conclusions and argued no extreme case with "partial witnesses", nor could it remotely be described as "trial by television" – Tom King's phrases yesterday in the Commons. It simply raised serious questions and suggested that they required deep examination.

'The questions were many. Were the terrorists challenged before they were shot? Did they attempt to surrender? Could they have been arrested? Was there any evidence for the belief that their car contained explosives? Why were they not stopped earlier? In the most controversial part of the programme, *This Week* brought forward witnesses – two on camera, one hidden from view and one in a written statement – who gave accounts of the killings. One of them, Carmen Proetta, suggested that the terrorists had attempted to raise their hands in surrender, and no one could be found to say that the terrorists had been challenged.

'A contrary opinion, however, was not suppressed: one expert, Lieutenant Colonel George Stiles (sic), a former bomb disposal officer, said that the gesture of surrender could also have been a reaction to the first shots which hit. But he also suggested that the operation was aimed at eliminating the terrorists "quickly and cleanly".

'Perhaps the final testimony to the fairness of the programme was that we were left with the feeling that the killings could have been necessary and justifiable; but without the examination of witnesses and evidence it is impossible to say.'

Chapter Six

Making the programme
I: tracking the terrorists

62 As a preliminary to our consideration of how the programme was compiled we summarize the events which took place in Gibraltar on Sunday, 6 March 1988. A plan of the location where the shootings occurred is printed at the end of this chapter.

63 The three persons acknowledged by the Provisional IRA to have been on active service when they were shot dead on 6 March were Daniel McCann, Mairead Farrell and Sean Savage. Savage entered Gibraltar some time between 12:30 and 1:00 pm on 6 March in a white Renault 5 car which had been hired in Spain. He parked the car in an area known as Ince's Yard. It was here that soldiers of the Royal Anglian Regiment assembled for the guard-mounting ceremony on Tuesday mornings, and where they re-assembled when the ceremony was over. It is an enclosed area, bounded on the north and west sides by high buildings, and on the south side by one of Gibraltar's massive old defensive walls. The east side opens onto Main Street. A single rank of public car-parking spaces runs along the old wall. McCann and Farrell entered Gibraltar on foot at about 2:30 pm on 6 March. Some time after 3 pm, the three terrorists met near the white Renault and at about 3:30 pm started to make their way back towards Spain on foot. By this time, at least, they were all under surveillance. At about 3:40 pm, McCann and Farrell had reached the Shell petrol station on the east side of Winston Churchill Avenue, a dual-carriageway road running northwards towards the Spanish border. They were on the pavement on the east side of Winston Churchill Avenue, walking towards Spain. Savage had parted from the other two and was heading back towards the centre of Gibraltar via Corral Road at the southern end of Winston Churchill Avenue. The precise details of what happened next are not clear, and probably never will be. It

appears to be generally agreed, however, that the first thing that occurred was that a police car which was stationary near the Winston Churchill Avenue end of Smith Dorrien Avenue sounded its siren. Almost immediately, a number of shots were fired at McCann and Farrell. They died on the pavement in front of the Shell station. Savage had meanwhile turned off Corral Road, going up the track known as Landport Ditch. There he was shot several times and died under an old ilex tree. By 3:45 pm, all three terrorists were dead, the sequence of events having occupied less than three minutes. The men who fired the shots were four SAS soldiers in plain clothes.

64 The following afternoon, Monday, 7 March, the Foreign Secretary made a statement about the shootings in the House of Commons. The full text is printed in paragraph 83 at the end of this chapter. Two particular aspects of his statement stood out. First, there was the revelation that the terrorists had been unarmed. Second, the Foreign Secretary stated that, contrary to earlier reports, no bomb had been found in the white Renault parked in Ince's Yard. It was these two features in particular that suggested to Bolton the Gibraltar shootings as a possible subject for a THIS WEEK programme. He discussed his thoughts with Oxley and Manyon on the evening of 7 March. On 8 March, he put the proposal to Sales and obtained his agreement in principle. As we have noted in chapter Three (paragraph 30), Sales had been particularly struck by the Foreign Secretary's announcement that the terrorists were unarmed, which seemed to him to raise the question why, if it were so, the terrorists should have made what were said to have been threatening movements. Bolton told us that he had been impressed by a leading article in the *Daily Telegraph* on 8 March, drawing attention to the fact that Government spokesmen had given a number of apparently contradictory accounts of the shootings.

65 On 8 March, Oxley and Manyon, diverted from Japan (chapter Three, paragraph 32), went to Gibraltar and Spain. These two early visits were in the nature of reconnaissance expeditions.

Oxley was to investigate what evidence relating to the shootings might be found in Gibraltar. Manyon was to make inquiries in Spain to try to discover how far the terrorists had been kept under surveillance by the Spanish authorities before they entered Gibraltar and what information might have been relayed by the Spanish to the British authorities.

66 Manyon's trip to Spain was prompted by the terms of the Foreign Secretary's statement on 7 March. In it he had expressed the Government's gratitude to the Spanish authorities for their assistance and co-operation, without which he said 'the outcome might have been very different'. He said that one of the terrorists (Savage) brought a white Renault 5 into Gibraltar 'shortly before 1 pm' on 6 March and 'was seen to park it in the area where the band for the guard mounting ceremony assembles'; and that 'an hour and a half later, the two others (McCann and Farrell) . . . were seen to enter Gibraltar on foot'. To the THIS WEEK team these statements suggested that the British and Gibraltar authorities knew when the terrorists had entered Gibraltar, had kept them under surveillance thereafter, and that their preparedness owed something to the Spanish authorities.

67 On 8 March, Manyon went to Malaga, moving on to Madrid on 11 March where he enlisted as consultant and interpreter Harry Debelius, an American journalist who had lived and worked in Spain for many years and contributed articles on Spanish affairs to English newspapers, notably *The Times*. On 14 March, Manyon and Debelius met Sr Manuel Jimenez Cuevas, chief of press and public relations for the Spanish police. They asked Sr Cuevas if he would be willing to provide details of the Spanish surveillance operation and to give a filmed interview. He indicated that he would, but asked Manyon and Debelius to make a formal request in writing.

68 This they did, by letter dated 15 March. Manyon gained the impression from his meeting with Sr Cuevas that the Spanish

authorities had kept the terrorists under continuous surveillance while they were in Spain and the British authorities informed of the terrorists' movements. While he was in Spain, Manyon also obtained a communique issued by the Spanish Interior Ministry on 9 March, which stated that 'for more than five months members of the Spanish and British police have kept close watch on the terrorists'. That information appeared to be consistent with earlier reports in English newspapers. For example, on 8 March, the *Independent* had reported that the Spanish police had kept the three terrorists 'under constant surveillance' and quoted an unnamed Spanish police source as saying 'we followed their steps right up to Gibraltar's gate'; while, on the same day, the *Daily Telegraph* had reported as a fact that the Spanish police had tailed the white Renault 5 'right up to the gate; on the other side the Gibraltarians took up the tail'.

69 In Gibraltar, Oxley met Stephen Bullock and Mrs Josie Celecia, both of whom had already given detailed interviews to GBC and the English newspapers. He also discovered two other people who said they had seen the shootings at the Shell station. One, Derek Luise, gave an account of the shootings which was similar to Stephen Bullock's. The other man refused to give his name (and later proved impossible to trace). Oxley also spoke to the Gibraltar Coroner, Felix Pizzarello, who told him that journalistic inquiries could be useful in helping to trace witnesses for the inquest.

70 Oxley returned to London on 11 March and Manyon on 14 March. On 15 March, they discussed their preliminary findings with Bolton. Oxley also reported two general impressions he had gained while in Gibraltar. He had sensed that local people were reluctant to discuss the shootings in detail: it was his feeling that they were nervous and afraid to do so. He had also formed the impression that the way in which the Gibraltar police had carried out their inquiries into the incident had not been as thorough as it might have been.

71 In the light of these preliminary researches Bolton authorized filming to begin, but with two reservations. The first was the question of payment which we have dealt with in chapter Three (paragraph 43). The second arose from Bolton's belief that the only way to ascertain whether there was enough substance for a programme was to carry out painstaking door-to-door inquiries in Gibraltar. He accepted that these inquiries might lead to nothing of value, in which case filming might have to be abandoned. Consequently 'authority to begin filming' does not mean that a programme will necessarily result. What it does mean is that the Editor is willing to commit technical and financial resources to a project which may, but will not always, come to fruition.

72 Chronologically, the next stage was the filming in Northern Ireland at the funeral of the deceased terrorists. The details of this have already been described in chapter Three. The following day, 17 March, Oxley, Manyon and a film crew left for Gibraltar. On 18 March, an interview was filmed with Stephen Bullock and on 19 March, Josie Celecia and her husband Douglas were interviewed, in each case by Manyon. Alison Cahn, the researcher, joined the team in Gibraltar on 18 March, but took no part in the interviews with Bullock or the Celecias. Her role in the production process is described in the next chapter. Both Bullock and Mrs Celecia had already given detailed accounts of what they had seen on GBC and in the English newspapers (see, for example, in Mrs Celecia's case, the *Daily Mail* of 7 March and, in Bullock's case, *The Times* of 8 March). They had also both given statements to the Gibraltar police.

73 On the afternoon of 6 March, Stephen Bullock, an English barrister practising in Gibraltar, was taking a Sunday walk along Smith Dorrien Avenue towards Spain with his wife and young child. They were on the east side of Smith Dorrien Avenue, near its junction with Winston Churchill Avenue. The traffic in Smith Dorrien Avenue was stationary. A police car close by the

Bullocks turned on its siren, swung out of the traffic and made towards the Shell station on the wrong side of the road. Almost immediately, the shooting at the petrol station began. Bullock looked in that direction. What he saw is set out in his own words in the transcript of the programme (chapter Four, pages 28, 36, 54–55).

74 Mrs Celecia and her husband Douglas live in a flat in George Jeger House, part of the Glacis Estate, one of the housing estates which form an amphitheatre round the Shell station. George Jeger House is on the west side of Winston Churchill Avenue, opposite the petrol station. It is set at an angle to the road, and the Celecias' flat forms the northern corner of the first floor. It has two windows overlooking the petrol station. Those windows are about 50 feet from where McCann and Farrell were shot. On the afternoon of 6 March, Mrs Celecia was looking out of her window towards the petrol station. She noticed two people walking towards Spain (in fact, McCann and Farrell). She looked away from them, towards the adventure playground on the northern (Spanish) side of the petrol station. Then she heard shots, and looked back. The account she and her husband gave of what they saw and heard is contained in the transcript (chapter Four, pages 51–52 and 55–56).

75 Although the programme transcript is limited to those parts of the interviews which were included in the completed programme, we have scrutinized the unedited transcripts of everything that was said on film by Bullock and the Celecias. We have also seen Bullock and Mr Celecia ourselves in Gibraltar. Mrs Celecia was unwilling to meet us. Her husband told us that she was a shy and somewhat nervous person whose tolerance of interrogation about what she had seen was exhausted. We have no reason to doubt this. On the basis of our inquiries we are satisfied that the accounts which Bullock and Mrs Celecia gave to THIS WEEK were substantially the same as those which they had given previously. We do not consider that any attempt was made by Manyon to trick, lead or bully them into saying anything

other than what they believed to be the truth. Both Bullock and
Mr Celecia volunteered the opinion that the behaviour of the
THIS WEEK team had been entirely proper, and each of them
confirmed that no payments had been received from anyone
connected with THIS WEEK. With two exceptions (to which
we return in chapter Eight), we have concluded that the completed programme fairly represented the true significance of
their evidence.

76 On 20 March, Oxley, Manyon and the film crew went on to
Spain, and the following day Manyon and Debelius were in
Madrid. They spoke again to Sr Cuevas of the Spanish police,
and later in the day, 21 March, had a meeting lasting one and a
half hours at the Interior Ministry with Sr Agustin Valladolid,
director of the press office for the Secretary of State for
Security. The journalists have told us that Sr Valladolid spoke in
Spanish from detailed notes, from time to time using the telephone to check points arising in the course of discussion.
Manyon asked questions in English and Debelius then trans-
lated them into Spanish and the answers into English. Later
Debelius spoke to Sr Valladolid by telephone to clarify some
details. Manyon also obtained a written statement from police
headquarters at the Interior Ministry. From these sources,
Manyon and Debelius constructed an account of the part the
Spanish authorities had played in keeping the three terrorists
under continuous surveillance and the British authorities
informed about their movements.

77 It was this account that formed the basis of the scenes in the
programme depicting the IRA unit meeting up in Marbella and
setting out for Gibraltar in two separate cars, both under surveillance by what the commentary described as 'plain clothes
officers of Spain's elite anti-terrorist squad'. A re-enacted film
sequence showed the white Renault driven by Savage and a red
Ford Fiesta containing McCann and Farrell being trailed from
Marbella to La Linea, the Spanish town which lies at the border
with Gibraltar. The white Renault was under observation right

up to the border check-point. The red Fiesta was parked in La
Linea, and McCann and Farrell were allowed to enter Gibraltar
on foot. The programme demonstrated how the Spanish
authorities had used up to four unmarked cars to track the
terrorists' progress all the way to La Linea. The unmarked
police cars constantly interchanged positions so as to avoid
arousing suspicion. With the co-operation and participation of
the Malaga police (two of the cars being driven by police officers
for the filming) this technique was reconstructed on the programme. In the commentary Manyon said he had been told by
the Spanish security police that a constant flow of information
about the terrorists' movements had been radioed directly to
British officials in Gibraltar and that a police helicopter made
sure the watchers made no mistake.

78 On 21 April, Manyon called on the Ministry of Defence in
London. He told us that among other matters he raised the
question of surveillance. The Director of Public Relations,
Army, who was at the meeting, told us he did not recall the issue
of surveillance being raised, but that he certainly would not have
discussed it in any detail. The Ministry's stated position on that
and other aspects had always been that it was not prepared to
give any information in advance of the inquest.

79 In the course of our Inquiry, we were provided with a copy of a
statement by a senior Spanish police officer which we were told
was prepared for use at the Coroner's inquest in response to a
Commission Rogatoire. In the event, it was not given in evidence, apparently because the Spanish Government was unwilling to agree that the officer should appear in person before a
court in Gibraltar. The deposition stated that all three terrorists
had been lost shortly after they had been sighted by the Spanish
police at Malaga airport on 4 March; that a thorough search of
the Costa del Sol on 5 and 6 March had failed to locate them;
and that the British and Gibraltar authorities had been advised
accordingly. This account from the Spanish side was similar to
the evidence given by British security service and Gibraltar

police witnesses to the inquest (which was not contested) that the terrorists had not been positively identified until they were already inside Gibraltar as a result of Savage being seen after parking the white Renault at Ince's Hall. Unknown to him the parking place was being watched as intelligence had indicated it was the likely location for the car bomb.

80 There is now, therefore, certain information emanating from official sources which conflicts with the account of surveillance given in the programme. Indeed the discrepancy between the programme's version of events and the evidence given at the inquest by witness O (a senior British security service officer), witness F (the senior military adviser), the Gibraltar Police Commissioner and a Detective Chief Inspector, was the first of the examples submitted to us by the Foreign Office in support of the criticism that the programme as a whole turned out to be significantly inaccurate. This issue underlines what we have said earlier in our report about hindsight.

81 The reality is that none of the information which became known at and after the inquest was accessible to the programme-makers at the time of the programme's production. The Ministry of Defence was unwilling to make any details available, whereas the Spanish authorities, through the channel of the appropriate spokesmen, had proved entirely co-operative. We have obtained confirmation from Madrid that Sr Valladolid did brief Manyon and Debelius on 21 March, although the Ministry of the Interior have no record of the terms in which he spoke. Debelius has sworn an affidavit in which he stated that during the interview on 21 March Sr Valladolid had said that on the day of the shootings, 6 March:

'... a white Renault car, which later came under suspicion as a car bomb, was under Spanish surveillance all the way down the coast road to its arrival in Gibraltar. The method of surveillance used was as follows:
(a) four or five police cars "leap-frogged" each other on the road while trailing the terrorists so as not to arouse suspicion.

(b) A helicopter spotted the car during part of the route.

(c) The police agents were in constant contact with their headquarters by radio.

(d) Observations by agents at fixed observation points along the road.

'Sr Valladolid further said that the Spanish police sent minute-by-minute details of the car's movements direct to the British in Gibraltar. He confirmed that the British were aware of the car's arrival at the border and permitted it to enter Gibraltar.'

82 The THIS WEEK journalists were not alone in believing that surveillance had been continuous. As mentioned in paragraph 68, both the *Daily Telegraph* and the *Independent* on 8 March had reported that the terrorists had been followed to the Gibraltar border, the latter quoting an unnamed Spanish police source to this effect. It may be that the press spokesmen in Madrid did not have full knowledge of all the operational details, but the journalists nevertheless went to the best sources available to them, and even succeeded in persuading the Malaga police to take part in a filmed reconstruction. There is no evidence to indicate that any contrary information was or could have been available at the time. In these circumstances, we do not consider that the use made of the information which had been obtained could fairly be characterized as unwarranted or irresponsible.

83 In reply to a private notice question in the House of Commons on 7 March 1988, the Secretary of State for Foreign and Commonwealth Affairs, Sir Geoffrey Howe, made the following statement on the shootings in Gibraltar:

'As the House will have heard, three identified terrorists, two men and one woman, were shot dead by security forces in Gibraltar yesterday afternoon. Two of them had a previous criminal record of terrorist activity. The IRA has since admitted that the three were members of an active service unit on active service in Gibraltar. The background and facts are as follows.

'Another known IRA terrorist, who was under surveillance by the Spanish authorities, recently crossed into Gibraltar and is thought to have carried out a reconnaissance for an act of terrorism. The activity undertaken suggested that the terrorist act might be in connection with the guard mounting ceremony, carried out on Tuesdays. The Gibraltar police were accordingly placed on high alert, and the police commissioner asked for military assistance in the light of his assessment of the threat.

'Shortly before 1 pm yesterday afternoon, one of those subsequently shot brought a white Renault car into Gibraltar and was seen to park it in the area where the band for the guard mounting ceremony assembles. Before leaving the car, he was seen to spend some time making adjustments in the vehicle. An hour and a half later, the two others subsequently shot were seen to enter Gibraltar on foot, and shortly before 3 pm joined the third terrorist in the town. Their presence and actions near the parked Renault car gave rise to strong suspicion that it contained a bomb, which appeared to be corroborated by a rapid technical examination of the car.

'About 3.30 pm, all three left the scene and started to walk back towards the border. On their way towards the border, they were challenged by the security forces. When challenged, they made movements which led the military personnel operating in support of the Gibraltar police to conclude that their own lives and the lives of others were under threat. In the light of this response, they were shot. Those killed were subsequently found not to have been carrying arms.

'The parked Renault car was subsequently dealt with by a military bomb disposal team. It has now been established that it did not contain an explosive device.

'Inquiries carried out by the Spanish authorities have matched keys found on one of the bodies with a Ford Fiesta car, subsequently found on the Spanish side of the border, which contained three false passports and items of equipment including insulating tape, electrical screwdrivers, a number of pairs of gloves, wire and an alarm clock. A key was also found for a third car. The search is continuing for this car and for explosives.

'An inquest will be held in Gibraltar.

'The suspect white Renault was parked in the area in which the band of soldiers would have formed for the Tuesday parade. A school and an old people's home were both close by. Had a bomb exploded in the area, not only the 50 soldiers involved in the parade, but a large number of civilians might well have been killed or injured. It is estimated that casualties could well have run into three figures.

'There is no doubt whatever that, as a result of yesterday's event, a dreadful terrorist act has been prevented. The three people killed were actively involved in the planning and attempted execution of that act. I am sure that the whole House will share with me the sense of relief and satisfaction that it has been averted.

'I am equally confident that the House will wish me to extend our gratitude to the Spanish authorities, without whose invaluable assistance the outcome might have been very different. This co-operation underlines once again the importance of international collaboration in the fight against terrorism.'

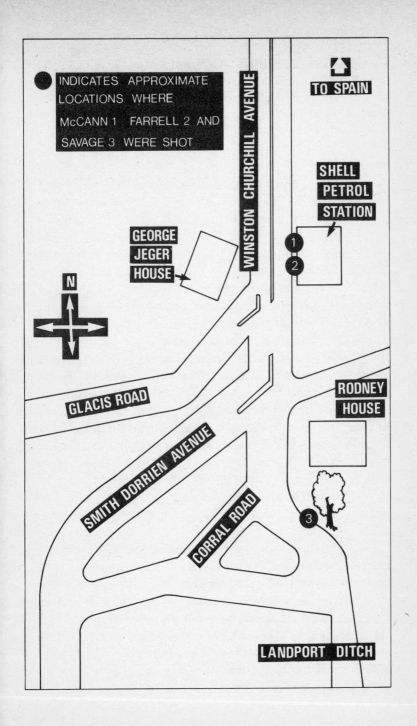

Chapter Seven

Making the programme
II: the exclusives

84 THIS WEEK found two exclusives in Gibraltar: an eyewitness named Carmen Proetta and a statement by a young bank clerk, Kenneth Asquez. They were to prove the most controversial contributors to the programme.

85 The researcher, Alison Cahn, had arrived in Gibraltar on 18 March. Her brief from Bolton was to conduct a systematic search for eyewitnesses to the shootings. She was to satisfy herself that the accounts given were honest, and to establish whether any witnesses were willing to give television interviews. The first person she saw was Derek Luise, whom Oxley had met on his previous visit (chapter Six, paragraph 69). Luise repeated his account to Alison Cahn, but in the end decided that he was not prepared to be filmed. Alison Cahn made attempts to trace the unnamed man whom Oxley had spoken to, but without success. She also followed up a hearsay account which had been given to Oxley. The substance of the account was that Farrell had her hands in the air when she was shot. Alison Cahn identified the author of the account, who confirmed the details through an intermediary, but refused to see either her or a lawyer.

86 Alison Cahn remained in Gibraltar until 31 March. During that time, she made extensive door-to-door inquiries in the blocks of flats surrounding the Shell station. She told us that she knocked on something approaching 150 doors, returning a second or third time if the occupants were out. Her abiding impression, like Oxley's, was that local people were afraid to speak about what they might have seen. One person she found who was willing to talk to her was Brian Delaney. He had not seen the actual shootings, only their immediate aftermath, and so was not

interviewed on film. His recollection of the appearance and positioning of the soldiers proved useful in verifying the accounts given by others.

87 On 27 March, while Colonel Styles was being interviewed on film at the Shell station, an elderly woman approached the production team and said that her daughter had seen the incident. She was the mother of Carmen Proetta. Alison Cahn went to see what Carmen Proetta had to say. Mrs Proetta was at first reluctant to recount the details of what she had seen. Gradually, however, the striking nature of her account became apparent. She then agreed to be filmed for the programme. Her interview was conducted by Manyon, in the presence of Colonel Styles.

88 Although living for part of the week in Spain, Mrs Proetta and her husband have a flat on the second floor of Rodney House to which she returns at weekends. Rodney House, which is part of the Laguna Estate, is set at right angles to the east side of Winston Churchill Avenue. The Proettas' flat looks out towards the Shell station about 90 yards away to the north. On the afternoon of 6 March, Mrs Proetta was in her kitchen washing up. The sink is by the window, which looks out over the Shell station. It was a warm afternoon and the window was open. She heard a police siren and looked out of the window. What she then saw is described in her own words in the transcript of the programme (chapter Four).

89 During one of the breaks in the filming, Colonel Styles put it to Mrs Proetta that the shots she believed had been fired by one of the soldiers crouching over the recumbent forms of McCann and Farrell had in fact been shots from the area of Corral Road, where Savage had been shot in Landport Ditch almost immediately after McCann and Farrell. Mrs Proetta rejected this possibility (the 'Corral Road' explanation). The track where Savage was shot lies behind Rodney House, whereas the Proettas' flat is at the front. Mrs Proetta remained convinced that the shots she heard all came from the Shell station in front of her.

90 At the end of her interview, Colonel Styles suggested to Mrs Proetta that the gesture of 'surrender' which she had seen the terrorists make might have been caused by the impact of the bullets and that, although she saw the gesture before she heard the shots, the true order of events was the reverse because light travels faster than sound. Mrs Proetta also rejected this possibility (the 'Colonel Styles' explanation). She was insistent that the terrorists had made a distinct movement, raising their hands to shoulder height or above, before any shots were fired.

91 Early on in their research, the THIS WEEK team had retained Christopher Finch, a lawyer in practice in Gibraltar, to advise on Gibraltar law and, if necessary to assist them in taking statements from witnesses. At this stage Finch, a former member of the Attorney-General's Chambers in Gibraltar, had not had any contact with the families of the deceased terrorists. It was not until May that he was instructed to assist the Belfast solicitor, Patrick McGrory, who represented the families at the inquest.

92 From the moment that she gave it, there was a realization that Mrs Proetta's account was likely to provoke controversy. The programme-makers were aware that they were the first people to whom she had spoken as she had not previously been in touch with either the police or the press. As a precaution, they took the unusual step of asking her if she would be willing to repeat her account in the form of a sworn statement. She agreed. On 29 March, therefore, Alison Cahn went with Finch to see Mrs Proetta in Spain. Finch took a statement from Mrs Proetta, which she later swore. It gave substantially the same account as her filmed interview. Before Alison Cahn left for the meeting with Mrs Proetta in Spain, Manyon asked her to put the 'Colonel Styles' explanation to Mrs Proetta again. She did so, and Mrs Proetta once again rejected it, explaining that, according to her recollection, the terrorists had their hands in the air for the 'couple of seconds or so' that it took the soldiers to take up their positions.

93 Both Colonel Styles and Finch were convinced that Mrs Proetta was telling the truth as she believed it to be. Styles also informed the team that her statement that the soldiers who had fired the shots at McCann and Farrell had got out of a police car which had come from the direction of Spain and stopped just to the north of the Shell station on the west side of the road accorded with his own interpretation of what had happened. In his judgment, the nature and angle of the bullet marks on the petrol pumps in the Shell station indicated that the terrorists had been shot by persons standing in the road and firing from a position slightly to the north.

94 Mrs Proetta has given substantially the same account from the outset. The inference that two of the IRA terrorists were shot as they were trying to surrender was undoubtedly controversial, but we have found nothing to indicate that it represented anything other than the truth as she believed it to be. We have carefully scrutinized the whole of Mrs Proetta's interview by Manyon (including those parts of it which were not transmitted), and can find no trace of any attempt by her to exaggerate or embellish her evidence, or of any attempt by the interviewer to get her to do so. We have read the evidence Mrs Proetta later gave at the inquest, and we cannot see anything in it which casts doubt on the honesty of the account she first gave to the programme-makers. Finally, we have interviewed her ourselves.

95 In the light of sensational reports which had appeared in the British press (some of which led to proceedings for libel) we asked about her background. It emerged that there was no reason to think that she was motivated by 'anti-British' sentiments. Mrs Proetta told us that she had been born in Britain of a Gibraltarian father and a Spanish mother and that her children had been educated within the British system, partly in Gibraltar and partly in England. We also put to her in detail the various respects in which it might be said that her account was inaccurate or unreliable. In the result, while she was quite prepared to accept the possibility that she might have been mistaken in

some respects, she remained confident that she had seen what she said she saw. It is, of course, possible that Mrs Proetta is, as a matter of fact, mistaken in what she believes she saw. It is not our function to express a view about that. What is, however, clear to us is that she does not think so and, perhaps more important, that the account she gave to the programme-makers was that which she was convinced was the truth.

96 Diana Treacy was found on 28 March by Alison Cahn, who spoke to her first on the telephone and then met her at her place of work. Miss Treacy was interviewed at home on 29 March. Alison Cahn had gone to Spain with Finch to see Mrs Proetta, and it was left to Oxley and Manyon to visit Miss Treacy. Before filming the interview, Oxley and Manyon spent over an hour in discussion with her and her father, a retired Gibraltar police-man. Miss Treacy had already given a full statement to the police. Her father encouraged her to repeat that account to Oxley and Manyon. She consented, but was not willing to be identified. She therefore gave her interview back-to-camera and it was agreed that her name would not be mentioned on the programme. Her father assured Oxley and Manyon that the account she gave in the interview corresponded with what she had told the police. The portion of her interview which was broadcast is shown in the programme transcript (chapter Four, pages 57–58). We have examined the transcript of her entire interview and are satisfied that no attempt was made to lead her, and that she was allowed to give her own account in her own words of what she had seen. The completed programme also fairly represented the effect of her evidence.

97 Robert Randall is a third-generation Gibraltarian. He served for 30 years in the Gibraltar Regiment, rising through the ranks to Quartermaster, retiring with the rank of Major. In 1987 he received the MBE in recognition of his military services from HM The Queen at Buckingham Palace. He has been active in organizing sport for young people in Gibraltar, and is a well-known and respected figure in the community. Randall retired

from the Army in September 1986 and in March 1988 was employed by a construction company in Gibraltar. On the afternoon of 6 March he was at home in Nelson House on the Laguna Estate. He heard of the shootings from one of his sons, went out to see what had happened, and returned to his flat to fetch his video-camera. He then went back to the scene of the incident and recorded its aftermath.

98   Later that day, Randall was told that GBC had not managed to obtain any film of the incident and it was suggested that he should offer the station his video-recording. He did so. GBC accepted his offer and paid a small sum for its use. Parts of it were shown on GBC that evening and extracts were also shown, Randall told us, by CBS, ITN, BBC and Visnews. In due course, by arrangement with GBC, Major Randall said that he was paid a total of about £1700 for the broadcast use of his material, excluding the use by Thames. Randall also gave a recorded interview on GBC.

99   On the morning of 7 March, Randall called at the Algemene Bank in the course of his employment. One of the bank's employees was a 19-year-old clerk called Kenneth Asquez. Both he and his parents were known to Randall, and Randall had refereed football matches in which Kenneth Asquez had taken part since he was a boy. When Randall entered the bank, there was a group of about half-a-dozen people, customers and bank employees, standing by the counter where Asquez was working. Randall joined them. They were discussing the shootings. Asquez congratulated Randall on his video shots, which he had seen on television. Asquez then told Randall that he had seen one of the shootings. He said he had been in a car in Corral Road with his girl-friend, a man called Terence Poulson, and another woman. The car stopped, he said, and then he saw one man firing at another who was lying on the ground. According to Asquez, the man who was firing had his foot on the neck or chest of the man on the ground and was firing at his head. Asquez said that the man who fired the shots put a black beret on his head

and showed an identity card. The conversation between Asquez and Randall was conducted in Spanish.

100 On 22 March Alison Cahn telephoned Randall and later went to his home. Her purpose was to find out whether he would make his video-recording available to THIS WEEK. Parts of it were eventually used in the programme, for which Randall was paid the sums itemized in chapter Three, paragraph 44. The question of payment was not discussed between Randall and Alison Cahn on 22 March, but was agreed some time later between Randall and Oxley. At the same meeting Alison Cahn asked if Randall knew of anyone who had witnessed the shootings. He said that he did, and gave Alison Cahn an account of what Asquez had told him. He was not, however, prepared to reveal Asquez's identity or the identities of any of the others in the car with Asquez. Alison Cahn asked Randall whether he would be willing to contact the young man to find out if he would meet her and perhaps give an interview. Randall undertook to do so.

101 On the evening of 22 March, Randall telephoned Asquez, telling him of his conversation with Alison Cahn and asking him whether he would like to appear on television. Asquez replied that he did not think he would, because he did not want to get involved. On 23 March, Randall reported this conversation to Alison Cahn. She asked him to find out if the young man might be prepared to write down his account of what he had seen. On the morning of 24 March, Randall again spoke to Asquez on the telephone and told him that 'the lady from the television' had inquired whether he would be willing to provide a written statement of what he had seen. Asquez said that he was uncertain, but would think about it. The following day, 25 March, Asquez walked into Randall's office and handed him an account, in his own handwriting, of what he had seen. He had not signed it. Randall passed this handwritten statement to Alison Cahn. We have seen it. It is substantially the same account as Randall said he heard Asquez give in the Algemene Bank on 7 March.

102 Shortly afterwards, Alison Cahn discovered Asquez's identity from other sources – although she was never able to identify the other occupants of the car. On the morning of 30 March, she went to see Finch. She told Finch of Asquez's existence, and that he claimed to be a witness to one of the shootings. But she neither gave him a copy of Asquez's handwritten statement nor told him anything of its contents. The reason was that she was anxious to ensure that Asquez gave his account to Finch unprompted. Asquez's veracity could then be checked by comparing what he said to Finch with what he had said in his handwritten statement. Nor did she mention Randall or his role in the matter. She asked Finch to find out whether Asquez would be willing to make a formal statement. In her presence, Finch telephoned Asquez at his place of work.

103 Finch told Asquez that he was representing Thames Television and asked if he would be willing to come to his chambers to make a statement about what he had seen. Asquez agreed to do so, but made it clear he was not willing to be filmed for television. Finch left the matter there. During his lunch-hour, Asquez came to Finch's chambers. Finch told us that Asquez gave his account slowly and quietly, responding to occasional questions. Finch took notes of what Asquez was saying. Asquez appeared to accept, Finch told us, that his account could be used on television, so long as he was not identified. Finch later put his notes into the form of a draft affidavit. Asquez was then telephoned from Finch's chambers and asked to come and sign the document. He refused. The notes of the interview record Asquez as having said that he was frightened that 'people would get him' if he became involved.

104 The same afternoon, Finch met the production team and told them what had happened. He believed that Asquez had been telling the truth, and that the fact Asquez had been willing to repeat his story in a lawyer's chambers enhanced its credibility. Finch also said that, although Asquez was not willing to sign the statement, he had accepted that it could be used in the programme so long as he was not identified. We have seen the

original of Finch's contemporaneous notes of his interview with Asquez, and we have been provided with copies of these notes and of the draft affidavit which Finch later prepared. The draft affidavit is an accurate reflection of the notes. Moreover, both give substantially the same account as the handwritten statement which Asquez had given to Randall.

105 By now it is notorious that Asquez retracted important parts of his statement when he came to give evidence at the inquest. He said that the reason why he made the statement in the first place was that he had been harassed and pressured by Randall, who had hinted that he could expect to benefit financially. We have interviewed Major Randall ourselves. He struck us as an intelligent man with a strong personality. He recounted his role substantially as it is set out above. While it is conceivable that Asquez might have felt some desire to oblige Major Randall, we have found nothing to suggest that Randall sought to persuade Asquez against his will, or that he made any offer or suggestion of financial reward.

106 At this point we must disclose that we were no more successful than the THIS WEEK team in making contact with the elusive Mr Asquez. We invited him to meet us when we visited Gibraltar, but his lawyer, Sir Joshua Hassan QC, replied that his client was reluctant to do so. Sir Joshua, the former Chief Minister, added that he personally wished to assist the Inquiry in any way possible, and we acknowledge the courteous and frank way in which he answered our questions about this perplexing affair.

107 We also met Mr Finch, who was similarly co-operative. He told us, as he had told the programme-makers, that in his judgment Asquez was telling the truth when he came to see him at the end of March. Finch is an experienced trial lawyer, accustomed to interviewing witnesses and assessing their credibility. Nothing we heard in Gibraltar indicated that Asquez's attendance at Finch's chambers was involuntary, or that Finch conducted the interview in anything but a correct professional manner.

108   One of the most forceful criticisms of 'Death on the Rock' concerned the use to which Asquez's statement was put in the programme. The first limb of that criticism is that the statement should never have been used at all. Three reasons have been advanced in support of that argument. The first is that the statement constituted a grave accusation against one of the soldiers. The second is that the programme-makers had not interviewed Asquez themselves nor even met him, so that they had not had any opportunity of assessing his credibility for themselves. The third is that they knew he had refused to swear or sign the statement, indeed that he had not even seen it in draft form. For these reasons, it is claimed, it was irresponsible to use the statement at all.

109   The programme-makers' response is as follows. Asquez had volunteered his original handwritten statement to Randall. They were aware that the handwritten statement corresponded with what, according to Randall, Asquez had told him in the bank on the day after the shootings. There was no reason to doubt the integrity of Randall. They knew that Asquez had agreed to come to Finch's chambers and had agreed to be interviewed by Finch, the legal representative of THIS WEEK. They knew that Finch had not seen the handwritten statement and was unaware of its contents; yet they could see that the two statements gave sub-stantially the same account. They had no reason to distrust Finch's account of the way in which Asquez had behaved or his judgment of Asquez's credibility. Finally, they asked themselves the question why, if it were untrue, Asquez should have invented such an horrific story. In the light of these considerations, it was in our judgment reasonable for the programme-makers to place some reliance on Asquez's statement.

110   But that conclusion does not dispose of this criticism in its entirety. What underlies it is the perception that the programme accused the soldiers of murder. If that were so, then, despite all the factors set out above, it would clearly have been quite wrong to use the Asquez statement as support for such a serious

accusation. If, however, as we have found in chapter Five, the programme did not make such an accusation, but rather pointed towards the possibility that the terrorists had been unlawfully killed, then it seems to us that it was, on balance, legitimate to refer to the Asquez statement as one of the sources which suggested that possibility.

111 The second charge is that the way in which Asquez's statement was presented in the programme gave it a spurious credibility. It is claimed that the programme's failure to make explicit that Asquez had refused to sign the statement, and had not even seen it, deprived the viewer of an essential qualification to its credibility. There is force in this criticism. The answer which the programme-makers give is that if those qualifications had been expressed, then it would have been necessary to explain the reasons why Asquez had refused to sign his statement, and to set out in full all the circumstances which had led them to conclude that his refusal to sign the statement, and the fact that he had not seen it, did not significantly affect its credibility. We do not find that answer entirely convincing. We think it would have been preferable to have given a fuller account of the circumstances in which such an unusual piece of evidence had been obtained and of the reasons for its inclusion in the programme. If that had been done, the viewer would have been better equipped to form his own conclusions about the true weight and significance to be attached to what was, as the commentary implicitly recognized, a dramatic account of a deliberate act of murder.

Chapter Eight

Making the programme
III: the detailed criticisms

112 Before moving on to consider a number of detailed criticisms which have been made of the commentary, we pause here to note what the Coroner said about evaluating the evidence of eyewitnesses in his summing-up. He told the jury that in order to gauge the credibility, truth and accuracy of a witness they should look further than demeanour. He went on:

'You will test the evidence of a witness against the evidence as a whole to see if it is accurate and true. For this you will look at the discrepancies which the evidence has thrown up. Discrepancies are of two kinds: one when the witness on his own account says things which are seemingly not consistent; the other, discrepancies which are thrown up on a comparison of each witness's story. It is for you to judge these. Are the discrepancies important? Are they minor? Are they explicable? Are they relevant?

'You will remember and keep in mind when considering these matters that it is of the very nature of man that things which happen even to oneself are not recalled in their totality. One forgets. One gets confused. The matter under review, let me remind you, took place six months ago, and it is essential to remember that the important acts took place in under three minutes, and the essential matters occurred in the space of, I believe – but it is a matter for you – less than thirty seconds from the moment of the split of Savage from the others at the junction of Smith Dorrien Avenue and Corral Road to their deaths.'

113 Two specific criticisms have been directed at a passage in the commentary which appears on page 51 of the programme transcript in chapter Four. This reads as follows:

'We have interviewed four key witnesses to the shootings. Their accounts raise serious questions about what really happened that afternoon, for they say that the British soldiers opened fire without warning, and none of them saw the IRA bombers make any threatening movements.'

114 Of the four eyewitnesses whose filmed interviews were included in the programme (Bullock, Mrs Celecia, Mrs Proetta and Miss Treacy), it is claimed that only Mrs Proetta said that no warnings were given before the soldiers opened fire; and that neither Bullock nor Mrs Celecia was asked whether they heard any warning or challenge. It is also claimed that Miss Treacy said merely that she heard no warning, not that the soldiers opened fire without warning.

115 These criticisms are based on those parts of the filmed interviews which were included in the programme. Our examination of the transcripts of the unedited interviews revealed that all four of the eyewitnesses were asked by Manyon whether they heard any warning or challenge before the soldiers opened fire. In Mrs Celecia's case, the question was:

'Before the shots, before you knew anything was happening, did you hear any kind of warning – any kind of command to stop?'

Her answer was:

'Nothing. No. I only heard those two shots.'

What Mrs Celecia said she saw was two people, later identified as McCann and Farrell, on the pavement by the Shell station opposite her flat, that she looked away momentarily, and then looked back again when she heard the first shot. The window of her flat was only about 50 feet from the Shell station. The programme-makers had been told by various people that Winston Churchill Avenue was empty of traffic, and therefore presumably quiet, at the time of the incident. In those circumstances, we do not think it was misleading to represent the totality of Mrs Celecia's evidence by the words 'they say that the British soldiers opened fire without warning'. Fairly interpreted, we think that was the effect of what Mrs Celecia had told the interviewer, even though the actual question and answer were not included in the programme as broadcast.

116 The same does not apply to the evidence of Bullock. The question Manyon asked him was:

'As you looked towards the petrol station first of all, had you heard any kind of warning, any shouted command or warning?'

His reply was:

'The first thing I heard was a volley of shots. That was what drew my attention.'

Thus, although it was true that Bullock had not heard a warning before the soldiers opened fire, it was equally clear that he was not in a position to say that none had been given. Indeed, given the distance between him and the Shell station, and the fact that he was standing beside a line of vehicles waiting at the traffic lights in Smith Dorrien Avenue, many of which will have had their engines running, it would have been surprising if he had been able to hear any warning or challenge, whether spoken or shouted, which might have been given. Bullock himself told us that this was the one aspect of the programme about which he had reservations. The commentary of the programme was written by Manyon, after extensive discussion with the other members of the team. When we put this point to him, he agreed that Bullock should have been excluded from the category of witnesses who were described as having said that the soldiers opened fire without warning. The other members of the THIS WEEK team also accepted this as an error, and Manyon said that he had apologized to Bullock for it shortly after the programme was transmitted.

117 In her interview Miss Treacy was asked about any warning, and this time the question and her answers were included in the

completed programme. She said that Savage had been shot in the back. The relevant part of the programme reads as follows (page 57 of the transcript):

Q: 'Did you hear any warning of any kind given by the man with the gun?'
A: 'No, no.'
Q: 'Did you hear him say: "Stop, police"?'
A: 'No, no. Just happened so sudden.'
Q: 'He just opened fire, just like that?'
A: 'Yes.'

Miss Treacy was very close to the shooting of Savage. The effect of her evidence was that no shots had been fired at Savage before those which she saw. In view of her proximity, we consider it to have been legitimate as a matter of inference to have included her in the category of witnesses who had said that the soldiers had opened fire without warning.

118 The second criticism which is made of the passage in the programme quoted in paragraph 113 is as follows. It is claimed that the passage implies that all four of the 'key witnesses' had said that they had not seen the terrorists make any threatening movements. We agree with that interpretation. The point is then made that Bullock, Mrs Celecia and Miss Treacy were never asked the question and expressed no view about it. In the case of Bullock and Mrs Celecia, the point is a fair one. They were not asked whether the terrorists had made any threatening movements. Nor, if they had been, would they have been in a position to express any opinion, since neither had seen the start of the shooting. Miss Treacy's situation is different. Her evidence was that Savage was shot in the back and without warning which seemed to preclude the possibility that he was shot because he had made threatening movements.

119 The programme-makers' first answer to this criticism is that this part of the commentary is literally true. So it is, but we do not

consider that a sufficient answer. The clear implication of the passage was that each of the four witnesses had stated positively that no threatening movements were made, which is not a fair reflection of the statements by Bullock and Mrs Celecia. The production team reply to that argument by drawing attention to the fact that the essential elements of each eyewitness's account were accurately put forward in the programme. In consequence, they say, it should have been apparent to the viewer that neither Bullock nor Mrs Celecia could have seen any threatening movements that might have been made. A close analysis of the transcript bears that out. Mrs Celecia says that she only looked back at the Shell station after she heard the first shots (pages 51–52 of the transcript) and Bullock's account is similar (pages 54–55). But that is an excessively pedantic approach to the question. Ordinary viewers of television programmes do not stop to consider whether the clear implications of the commentary are strictly supported by the evidence which is laid out in the programme. They do not have the advantage of a written transcript, nor do they have the time or the inclination to formulate reasoned arguments why this or that statement by the commentator may not stand up to close examination.

120 A third criticism which has been made relates to the following commentary passage (page 55 of the transcript):

'Looking from her window, Josie Celecia saw the terrorists on the ground, and an SAS man still pointing his pistol at them.'

It is claimed that Mrs Celecia does not actually say on the programme that she saw an SAS man point a pistol at the terrorist. Therefore, on this argument, it was not safe to assume that the second volley of shots she heard came from the man standing over McCann and Farrell: they could have been the shots from the Savage shooting (the 'Corral Road' explanation).

121 It is true that neither in the programme nor in any of the untransmitted parts of her interview did Mrs Celecia say that she

saw the SAS man holding a pistol. In an untransmitted part of her interview she said this:

'I didn't see any guns, but I heard the noise – it was coming from there (the Shell station).'

Manyon told us that he discussed this question with Mrs Celecia after her interview had been recorded and before he wrote the passage in the commentary which is set out in the preceding paragraph. She confirmed that she had seen a man standing over the fallen terrorists in what could be regarded as a firing position, and said she was certain that the second volley of shots she heard came from that direction as she looked. Manyon therefore concluded that the effect of Mrs Celecia's answer would be fairly represented by the form of words set out above. It was a matter of inference, but the plain effect of what she had said was that she believed she had seen an SAS man firing several shots at the recumbent terrorists. Thus, although it was incorrect to say that Mrs Celecia had actually seen a pistol, we do not think the inaccuracy materially misrepresented the true meaning of her evidence.

122 Colonel Styles told us that he had a reservation about the programme. Although he had expressed the view that it was likely to have been apparent to an expert eye that the white Renault did not contain a bomb, he had also told the THIS WEEK team that that did not exclude the possibility that there was another car with a bomb in it somewhere on the Rock, or else in La Linea. Colonel Styles explained this was a possibility of which the bomb disposal expert would have been aware. He was unhappy the possibility had not been canvassed on the programme, which he felt lacked balance as a result. He had written to THIS WEEK to tell them so shortly after the programme's transmission. We put this point to the production team. They told us they had considered including Colonel Styles' theory in the programme, but had in the end decided not to do so, because there was insufficient evidence to support it.

No suggestion had been made in any of the official statements that the authorities had suspected the existence of a bomb anywhere but in the white Renault, and the programme-makers found nothing in the course of their investigations to indicate the contrary. The THIS WEEK team point out that when there was backing for Colonel Styles' theories – for example, the 'Colonel Styles' explanation of what Mrs Proetta had described as a gesture of surrender (chapter Seven, paragraph 90) – they had been included in the programme.

123 We have found, therefore, that in two respects a key passage of the commentary was open to criticism (see paragraphs 113, 116 and 119). The Ministry of Defence have submitted that these faults demonstrate that 'the degree of scrupulousness displayed by the programme-makers was not commensurate with the gravity of the accusations implied against the soldiers'. We think that goes too far. In the first place, we repeat, we do not consider that the programme, taken as a whole, made accusations against the soldiers. More important, while we have no doubt that the passage in question was inappropriately worded, with the result that it misstated the effect of the evidence in two respects, we are not persuaded that that arose from any lack of scrupulousness. Indeed when the thoroughness of the research for the programme and the way in which the results were deployed are taken into account, the conclusion to be drawn is that the production team sought to obtain a wide range of evidence and to present it as fairly and accurately as possible. Examples to support that conclusion will be found in the earlier parts of this report. These lapses, therefore, although they cannot be dismissed as insignificant, need to be weighed against the programme overall.

124 The final component of the programme, an exposition of the primacy of the rule of law by George Carman, QC has attracted no criticism to our knowledge. Mr Carman explained that such force as is reasonable or reasonably necessary to prevent crime, in order to protect oneself or defend others, is justified in law.

But everything turns on the particular facts of the case. He went on to say:

'At the one extreme there is no unfettered licence to kill; at the other extreme, extreme danger requires extreme measures to be taken.'

Chapter Nine

The judicial process
I: prejudice

125 In its submission to our Inquiry the Foreign and Commonwealth Office raised two objections of principle. One was that the broadcast of 'Death on the Rock' might have had an undesirable impact on the inquest in Gibraltar, in particular because there was a risk that members of the inquest jury might have seen the programme or read about it, thus being influenced by what they had seen or read. This objection may be called the objection on the ground of prejudice. The other objection argued that the making of the programme, and its broadcast on 28 April, risked contaminating the evidence of witnesses who subsequently appeared at the inquest. We call this the objection on the ground of contamination.

126 Both Thames and the IBA sought the advice of Leading Counsel on the question whether the broadcast of the programme in the United Kingdom would constitute a contempt of court in relation to the inquest in Gibraltar. Both received unequivocal opinions that it would not. We agree with those opinions. It is difficult to see how a broadcast whose reception is confined to one jurisdiction could be said to constitute a contempt of proceedings taking place, or due to take place, in another jurisdiction. On the advice of one of its own lawyers Thames withdrew the sale of the programme to Gibraltar and Spain, and instructions were issued to Thames Television International accordingly. Two international news agencies, Visnews and WTN, were verbally advised that Thames was withholding the programme and that items from it should not be included in their services to Gibraltar or Spain. On the day of the broadcast ITN telephoned Sales in the first instance, speaking later to Bolton and Oxley, asking if they might tape the programme in advance of transmission in the light of the political controversy which was

blowing up. This request was agreed. Bolton pointed out, however, that although Thames had been advised the programme did
not raise an issue of contempt in the United Kingdom, ITN
should obtain its own legal advice over the international use of any
extracts. In the event ITN did not cover the story in its domestic
news bulletins on 28 April, but did include an item of approximately 2 minutes 20 seconds duration in *Super Channel News*.
This was a daily half-hour programme which at the time was
supplied by ITN under contract to Super Channel, a commercial
organization delivering a general programme service by satellite.
Several European cable companies received and relayed the
signal. Gibraltar Broadcasting (GBC) had a contract with Super
Channel enabling it to draw on this source for its regular nightly
news, and it was by this route that an extract from 'Death on the
Rock' was shown in Gibraltar on 28 April. When Thames became
aware of this transmission the following day, a telex was sent to the
General Manager of GBC stating that the transmission had been
without the agreement of Thames, stressing that the programme
was not available for showing in Gibraltar in whole or in part, by
extract or by repeating quotations from it.

127   The same day, Friday, 29 April, the Attorney-General of Gibraltar sought and obtained injunctions against the local press and
broadcast media effectively preventing them from broadcasting or
reporting any part of the programme which might prejudice the
inquest. The Attorney-General told us that he considered, but
decided against applying for similar injunctions against the
import, distribution or sale of English newspapers. Subsequently
it became evident that privately-recorded video cassettes of
'Death on the Rock' were imported from the United Kingdom
into Gibraltar. The controversy over the programme was reported
in the English newspapers, as were various statements made by
Ministers or official spokesmen at the Foreign Office or Ministry
of Defence.

128   The question which arises is whether it should have been fore-
seen that the programme, or crucial parts of it, would become

available in Gibraltar before the inquest and, if so, what effect that foresight should have had upon the decision to broadcast the programme. In our view, the likelihood of some 'seepage' of the programme into Gibraltar was foreseeable. The programme dealt with intensely controversial issues of great interest to Gibraltarians, many of whom have close links with this country. Since Gibraltar is a small and tightly-knit community, the possibility that potential jurors might see a cassette of the programme or an extract relayed by way of a satellite television service could not be discounted. Beyond that was the possibility of becoming aware of its nature and content in general terms from other sources, notably the English newspapers which gave extensive coverage to the broadcast.

129 It does not follow, however, that a potential juror's discharge of his or her duty at the inquest would have been significantly affected by what he or she had seen or heard of the programme. As we have explained in chapter Five, we do not consider that the programme asserted as a fact that the terrorists had been murdered. Rather its effect was to suggest that there was a real possibility that the terrorists had been unlawfully killed. This proposition was always likely to be raised at the inquest (as in due course it was). The test, it seems to us, is whether there was a *real* risk that the proceedings of the inquest would be adversely affected.

130 We do not believe there was. Our first reason for that judgement is that we do not think the programme was likely to predispose fair and reasonable jurors to decide the factual issues at the inquest in any particular way. True, they might fairly say of the programme, it presented the possibility of unlawful killing in a vivid and dramatic form. At the same time, however, it would, we think, be evident to them that it was only one of the possible explanations. They would be aware they had not heard the soldiers' or the Gibraltar police's account, nor the evidence of other eyewitnesses, and that they would not do so until the inquest took place. To be conscious of a possibility, however

vividly presented, should not, for the ordinary, fair-minded man, be the same as to be convinced that it is the truth, or even that it is more likely than not to be the truth.

131 We acknowledge that potential jurors who had not seen the programme, but who had read certain accounts of it in the English newspapers (for example, in the *Sun*, the *Daily Mail* or the *Daily Express* on 29 April 1988) might have been left with the impression that the programme had asserted as a fact that the terrorists had been murdered. But we are unable to accept that as a fair interpretation of the programme; and we do not consider that the programme-makers (or the IBA) can be held responsible for a portrayal of the programme in other media which was neither obvious nor intended.

132 Even if it were to be the case that the programme was more strongly suggestive of the 'murder' thesis than we believe it was, and that, in consequence, it had a real tendency to predispose potential jurors to decide the issues at the inquest in a particular way, we do not consider there was any significant risk that such a predisposition was likely to survive the detailed examination of the evidence which the inquest was bound to involve, so influencing the final verdict.

133 In common with the authorities cited below, we have faith in the ability of juries to leave extraneous influences outside the jury-box, and to decide the disputed matters before them on the evidence and arguments presented to them in court by the witnesses and the advocates which are summarized, with appropriate directions on the law, by the judge. The Master of the Rolls has recently pointed out that:

'... for one reason or another a trial, by its very nature, seems to cause all concerned to become progressively more inward-looking, studying the evidence given and submissions made to the exclusion of other sources of enlightenment. This is a well-known phenomenon. As Lawton J put it on the basis of vast experience of jury trials, both at the

Bar and on the Bench: "the drama, if I may use that term, of a trial almost always has the effect of excluding from recollection that which went before": *Reg.* v. *Kray* (1969) 53 Cr App R 412, 415.'
A G v. *News Group Newspapers Ltd* [1987] QB 1,16, per Sir John Donaldson MR

In the Kray case, Lawton J also said this:

'I have enough confidence in my fellow-countrymen to think that they have got newspapers sized up and they are capable in normal circumstances of looking at a matter fairly and without prejudice even though they have to disregard what they may have read in a newspaper.'
Reg. v. *Kray*, supra, 414.

134 Whenever issues of fact are to be decided by a jury, irrespective of the nature of the tribunal, instances may arise in which publication before, or during, the proceedings will create a risk of prejudice which is ineradicable, however strongly the jury is urged to ignore what they may have read or seen and to concentrate on the evidence and arguments laid before them. An obvious case is where a publication reveals that a person who is being, or is about to be, tried for a criminal offence has previous convictions. Another case, superficially more relevant to this Inquiry, is where a publication suggests that a person who is on trial or about to stand trial is guilty of the offence with which he is charged.

135 Although an inquest is not a trial, and the coroner is not necessarily judicially experienced, the Gibraltar inquest was conducted by a resident judge of first instance and bore all the marks of a properly conducted judicial process. It began on 6 September 1988 and lasted 19 days, during which time much new information about the incident was brought to light. The coroner gave his summing-up on 30 September. He directed the jury of 11 men that there were three verdicts open to them: a verdict of 'killed unlawfully'; a verdict of 'killed lawfully'; or an open verdict. He told the jury that a verdict of unlawful killing would

be appropriate if they found that the soldiers had used force when it was not necessary, or had used more force than was reasonably necessary; or if they found that the soldiers had been 'unwitting tools of a plot to dispose of the three suspects'. He directed the jury that a verdict of 'killed unlawfully' would require them to be satisfied beyond reasonable doubt that that was so. Otherwise, he said, the verdict should be 'killed lawfully'. He urged them to avoid an open verdict and to be unanimous. After a retirement lasting seven and three quarter hours, and by a majority of nine to two, the jury found that the terrorists had been killed lawfully.

136 The purpose of the Gibraltar inquest was to establish the cause of the death of the deceased, and not to convict or acquit the soldiers who shot them. Nevertheless the probability was that a finding of unlawful killing would have been followed by criminal charges. So the stakes were undoubtedly high, and it is right to review the possible impact of 'Death on the Rock' on the Gibraltar jury with the utmost seriousness. At the time of the broadcast no date for the inquest had been set, and it was still not known whether the soldiers would give evidence. The programme was screened against the background of a welter of public comment about the shootings, one element of which had canvassed the possibility of unlawful killing. Other comment, however, tended to endorse the account given by the Foreign Secretary in the House of Commons on 7 March, whose tenor was that the terrorists had been lawfully killed. It was inevitable that, before reaching their verdict, the jury would spend a considerable length of time absorbed in a mass of detailed evidence and argument in which conflicting explanations of the shootings would be exhaustively examined. In those circumstances, we do not believe there was any real likelihood that whatever a member of the jury might have seen or heard of the programme would have overridden the more immediate and powerful effects of the proceedings at the inquest.

137 For these reasons we conclude that 'Death on the Rock' did not create any real risk of prejudice, and that there is no persuasive reason why the programme-makers or the IBA should have anticipated that it might.

Chapter Ten

The judicial process
II: contamination

138 The nature of the objection on the ground of contamination is this: if people who have witnessed events which are the subject of forthcoming judicial proceedings are interviewed for television, there is a danger that the value of their evidence to the tribunal which is appointed to investigate and adjudicate upon those events may be undermined; and the danger may be increased if the interviews are broadcast before the proceedings take place. The danger may arise in a number of ways:

- a witness may be tricked, led or bullied by the interviewer into giving a false or misleading account of the events in question;

- a witness may give a deliberately false account, either for ulterior purposes of his own, or for money, or because he is tempted into exaggeration by the prospect of publicity;

- a witness may give what he genuinely believes to be an honest account, but one which is, in fact, inaccurate.

139 One of the potentially damaging consequences for the administration of justice is that a witness who has been interviewed on television may be unwilling to accept that the account he has already given for public consumption is inaccurate or misleading. If that account was, indeed, inaccurate or misleading, then there is a danger that the tribunal may be misled by the witness's adherence to it. We describe this as contamination by *crystallization*. Alternatively, when he gives evidence, a witness may be willing to accept that his earlier account was inaccurate, in which case his credibility, and hence the value of his evidence as a whole, may be undermined. If so, and if the account which he has given to the tribunal was indeed accurate, the tribunal may be deprived of a valuable aid in making its decision. We

describe this as contamination by *discredit*. In an extreme case, either form of contamination could lead the tribunal to make a wrong decision, so causing injustice to one or more of the interested parties.

140 Some of these issues were considered in 1969 by an Inter-departmental Committee under the chairmanship of Lord Justice Salmon which reviewed the law of contempt as it affected comments upon, or statements about, matters which had been referred to a Tribunal of Inquiry set up under the Tribunals of Inquiry (Evidence) Act 1921. In the aftermath of the Aberfan disaster in October 1966 various eyewitnesses who were potential witnesses to any inquiry were interviewed by the press before the resolutions had been passed in both Houses of Parliament, but after the Prime Minister had announced that an inquiry would be held. The Foreign Secretary referred to some recommendations of this committee in making his request that transmission of 'Death on the Rock' should be postponed, and we return to his intervention later in this chapter. The relevant paragraphs from the Salmon Committee's Report (Cmnd 4078) are set out at the conclusion of this chapter.

141 We accept that contamination by crystallization may occur in certain circumstances. But if a witness interviewed in advance of judicial proceedings has given his account voluntarily and honestly, without being tricked, bullied or led by the interviewer, without payment or other inducement, and without any ulterior motive to give a false account, then the danger of contamination by crystallization is much reduced.

142 It is a familiar human characteristic that people tend to adhere to the first account they have given, and that their adherence tends to become stronger as time passes. That is no doubt partly because people are naturally reluctant to withdraw or retreat from what they have first said, particularly when they have spoken thoughtfully about matters of importance and their words have been recorded and published. A second reason is

that memory fades. Consequently the law allows a witness to refresh his memory from his own contemporaneous record of what he observed, but will not allow him to use a record of his subsequent recollection. Contemporaneous accounts are inherently more reliable than subsequent recollection; the greater the passage of time, the less reliable recollection generally becomes. It is therefore not at all surprising that witnesses should tend to regard their earliest recollection of events as being the most reliable; adhering to the account they first gave with increasing conviction as time passes; responding to challenges to the accuracy of their recollection by referring, explicitly or subconsciously, to what they first said.

143 This well-observed phenomenon, however, does not necessarily entail any threat to the administration of justice. The account first given by an honest witness will often be a true account. Contamination can only occur if the administration of justice is adversely affected. No detriment to the administration of justice can be caused by the crystallization of an account which is, as a matter of fact, a true account. On the contrary, if it is a true account, then the interests of justice are likely to be advanced by the fact that the witness has been induced to adhere steadfastly to it, against all attempts to get him to alter or abandon it.

144 Any interview obtained and published in advance of a judicial hearing at which the person interviewed is likely to be a witness carries with it some risk that an inaccurate or mistaken account may become a fly in amber. But the crystallizing effect of a previous statement, whether published or made in private to the police or a solicitor, should not be overstated or elevated into a new ground for restricting comment on matters of public interest. Honest eyewitnesses who are aware that they will, or may, have to give evidence in judicial proceedings will be conscious of the risks to which they may be exposed if they give an account of events in advance of the hearing which is significantly different from what they later say to the tribunal. Such people should be conscious of the paramount obligation to tell the truth

in court as best they can, and will usually be prepared to acknowledge before the tribunal that an earlier account which they have given may be inaccurate in this or that respect. Only in rare cases will such an acknowledgement be likely to have a serious effect upon the credibility of the witness's evidence as a whole. Juries are well able to assess the credibility of witnesses, deciding how far the inconsistencies between two different accounts given by a witness are of any importance, and judging where, in the totality of a witness's evidence, the balance of truth is to be struck.

145 If those considerations are applied to an honest witness who has been interviewed in a fair and proper manner in advance of a judicial hearing, and whose interview has been recorded and published without distortion or misrepresentation, they suggest that the danger of contamination in such a case, though certainly not negligible, is perhaps rather less of a threat to the administration of justice than it may appear to be at face value. The same considerations also point to the conclusion that the risk of contamination by discredit is, in general, a less real threat than contamination by crystallization.

146 As rehearsed in the earlier chapters recounting the making of the programme, we have found no grounds to indicate that any of the four eyewitnesses (Stephen Bullock, Josie Celecia, Diana Treacy and Carmen Proetta) whose accounts were included in the programme were tricked, bullied or otherwise induced to say anything other than what they thought they had seen. Nor did we find anything to suggest that any of them might, for reasons of their own, have given false accounts to the programme-makers. Against this background of good faith we address two questions. First, was the fact that the witnesses had given an account of events to the programme-makers likely to have a significant effect on their evidence at the inquest? And second, was the broadcast of those accounts likely to compound that effect?

147 By the time they were interviewed by the programme-makers, three of the four eyewitnesses – Stephen Bullock, Josie Celecia

and Diana Treacy – had been interviewed by the Gibraltar police. Diana Treacy's father had assured the team that the account she gave to them was the same as that which she had given to the police. Two of them – Stephen Bullock and Josie Celecia – had also given detailed accounts which had been published in the media both in England and Gibraltar. The reported accounts in the press attributed to Bullock and Mrs Celecia were similar to what they said on the programme. It is a serious matter to give a detailed account to the police, or the press, of an incident as important as the Gibraltar shootings. Accordingly, whatever inaccuracies or inconsistencies there may have been in their accounts would have been likely to have been set in their minds before they were interviewed by the THIS WEEK team. In consequence, we doubt whether either the fact of being interviewed or the showing on television of those parts of their interviews which were included in the programme, could have made any appreciable contribution to the process of crystallization.

148 For the same reasons, we do not think it can be said that the obtaining and showing of the interviews of those witnesses created any appreciable risk of contamination by discredit. There was no reason to suppose that any of them was likely to depart significantly in what they said at the inquest from what they had said to the police, to the press and, subsequently, to THIS WEEK.

149 Before turning to the participation of Carmen Proetta and Kenneth Asquez, we refer back to the two questions posed in paragraph 146: the distinction between the risk of contamination which may result simply from the fact that a witness has given an account of events on a previous occasion, and the additional risk that may arise from the publication of that account. A person who first obtains the account of a material witness can hardly be criticized for having done so and for recording what the witness has to say. The administration of justice would be impaired if material witnesses went undiscovered or if, once discovered,

were left to give their first detailed account of events at a hearing which may take place months, or even years, after those events. The existence of Carmen Proetta and Kenneth Asquez became known as a result of the research carried out by THIS WEEK in Gibraltar. Neither had been identified as potential witnesses by the police, and it is probable that their evidence would not have emerged at all had they not been found during the preparation of the programme.

150 Mrs Proetta was traced through a chance meeting with her mother (see chapter Seven, paragraph 87). She was not paid, nor offered any payment. The programme-makers were conscious that her account was controversial and were careful to put to her the alternative explanations of what she had seen which we have referred to as the 'Colonel Styles' and 'Corral Road' explanations; she rejected both of them. Mrs Proetta came across as an intelligent and forceful person. She spoke to us on the record in a forthright and matter-of-fact manner. There is not in our view any reason to suppose that the account she first gave to the programme-makers was exaggerated or embellished by her for the sake of publicity or for any other reason, or that she was tricked or brow-beaten into saying anything other than what she believed to be the truth. This being so, we are led to the conclusion that there was no real risk that her participation in the programme might have significantly affected the substance of the evidence she was to give at the inquest, or the manner in which she gave it. In consequence, we do not believe that there was any real risk that her evidence would suffer contamination in either of its forms.

151 In chapter Seven we considered whether, as a matter of proper journalistic practice, the programme-makers were justified in using Kenneth Asquez's written statement and in presenting it in the way they did in 'Death on the Rock'. We now turn to the question whether the use to which Asquez's statement was put in the programme gave rise to the possibility of contamination. Although his identity was never revealed by the programme-

makers, or by Major Randall or Christopher Finch, it was foreseeable that, once the programme had been shown, Asquez would become known to the authorities, and that in consequence he might be called to give evidence as a witness at the inquest. This, indeed, was exactly what happened. To recapitulate the sequence of events: Asquez wrote out his story in manuscript and gave it to Randall, who passed it on to Alison Cahn. Later he repeated substantially the same account to Finch, who put it in the form of a draft affidavit. On each occasion, he knew that what he had to say was of interest to the programme-makers and might well appear on television. By the time he came to give evidence at the inquest, the crucial part of his story had been broadcast, although without attribution. Consequently it might be thought he would be subject to a natural inclination to stick to his original story.

152   The case of Kenneth Asquez differs from the others because none of the programme team had met him and had not therefore had the opportunity of assessing his credibility for themselves. Moreover, before the programme was broadcast, they knew that he had refused to swear or sign the statement he had given to Finch. Did these warning lights signal a real possibility that he might not have been telling the truth and might subsequently change his story? We preface our assessment of this possibility by observing that the damage to the administration of justice which may occur in such a case arises rather from the fact that the earlier statement has been made and then withdrawn, than from the fact that it has previously been published elsewhere. There may be cases in which the contents of a statement, or the circumstances in which it was obtained, or both, are such as ought to engender grave doubts about its credibility in the mind of the person who obtained it, but, for the reasons given below, we doubt that this was such a case.

153   The account given by Asquez was obviously controversial and dramatic and, although the programme-makers had not interviewed him themselves, they knew he had volunteered both the

handwritten statement which he gave to Randall and the statement taken by Finch. They also knew that Finch had not seen
the handwritten statement and was unaware of its contents; yet
they could see that the two statements gave substantially the
same account. Moreover, they had been told by Finch, whom
they had no reason to doubt, that in his judgement Asquez was
telling the truth as he saw it; and that he judged the value of the
statement to be enhanced by the fact that it had been made to
him in his office.

154 In those circumstances, it is questionable how far it was reasonable to expect that Asquez would retract his statement if he was
called to give evidence at the inquest. To point to the fact that, in
the event, this was just what he did do is to rely too heavily on
hindsight. Finally, as we have said, we do not in any case believe
that contamination by discredit is in general so real a threat to
the interests of justice as contamination by crystallization. In
support of that proposition (if we may, for once, be allowed a
little hindsight ourselves), we would invite attention to the fate
which befell Asquez's evidence at the inquest. Despite his
retraction of important parts of his earlier statement, the coroner
nonetheless left the whole statement to the jury as a version
which, on consideration of all the evidence, it was open to them
to accept if they thought it right to do so.

155 The other possibility was that Asquez's evidence might suffer
crystallization. But, given the contentious nature of the unsworn
statement, the circumstances in which it was obtained, and the
reluctance of Asquez to put his name to it, the likelihood was
that it would only be accepted if he gave evidence confirming it
in a convincing manner and if there was other credible evidence
to corroborate it. In that event, it is clear that any crystallizing
effect the programme might have had on Asquez's evidence
would have been immaterial.

Extract from the Report of the Interdepartmental Committee on the Law of Contempt as it affects Tribunals of Inquiry (Cmnd 4078, 1969)

The following paragraphs refer to contamination of evidence. They are reproduced with the permission of the Controller of Her Majesty's Stationery Office.

'29. The publication of interviews with prospective witnesses raises difficult problems. The Press, Television and Radio have always considered that once any type of tribunal has been appointed it is inappropriate for them to conduct anything in the nature of a parallel inquiry and they have never done so. We regard it as of the utmost importance that this restraint should continue to be exercised. Nevertheless the conducting of interviews as distinct from their publication should be permissible. This practice has been going on for years with the entirely legitimate object of obtaining background material for stories to be published after the appearance of the Tribunal's report. As a result of such interviews the Press has often rendered valuable public service by discovering fresh information and evidence which it has made available to the Tribunal. The question, however, is whether such interviews should be published in the Press or on Television or Radio after the Tribunal has been appointed and before it has reported. If, for example, the inquiry by Lord Denning in 1963 had taken the form of a Tribunal of Inquiry, although it would no doubt have had enormous news value, we think it would have offended everyone's sense of justice and propriety if say the late Dr Stephen Ward and Miss Christine Keeler had been interviewed on television the evening before they were to give evidence before the Tribunal. And yet there would have been nothing to prevent it except good taste and the law of contempt. One would not wish to see in this country the horror of trial by Press, Television and Radio. We are confident that the general public would deplore any alteration in our law which would permit such things to happen here. We have so far escaped them only because of a high sense of responsibility on the part of the Press, Television and Radio and also because of the law of contempt.

'30. It has been suggested that there should be a complete ban on such interviews being published. Up to now, we have got along without them very well and it has been widely assumed that the publication of such interviews, whatever form they might take, would amount to contempt. On the other hand it has not been seriously suggested that the publication of such interviews should be altogether unrestricted for it is generally recognised that they could be conducted in such a way as to contaminate the evidence. It is true that we have heard some faint suggestion that as witnesses are habitually interviewed and statements taken from them before they give their evidence, no great harm could result should they be interviewed on television before going into the witness box. The distinction, however, between being interviewed in the quiet of your own solicitor's office or by the Treasury Solicitor and being cross-examined under arc lights before an audience of millions by a skilled interviewer is perhaps not too fine to be appreciated without much difficulty by anyone of ordinary imagination and understanding.

'31. The real danger of such interviews is that witnesses whose evidence is vital to the matters under investigation are questioned without any of the safeguards which obtain in our courts of law or before Tribunals of Inquiry. We fully accept that the vast majority of those who would conduct such interviews are responsible and fair minded. But perhaps there are, or in the future may be, some exceptions to this general rule. A witness could be bullied or unfairly led into giving an account which was contrary to or put a slant upon the truth. He could commit himself, particularly under the strain and tension of a television interview, to a badly expressed or inaccurately recollected version of events. Witnesses might also be tempted to give a version of facts which they thought most newsworthy, particularly if a fee were being paid for the interview. When such witnesses came to give evidence before the Tribunal they would either have to stick to what they had already said, however inaccurate it might be, or reveal the true facts. In the latter event, the weight of their evidence might be considerably shaken by the discrepancy between what they were telling the Tribunal and what they had said previously. This might greatly hinder the Tribunal, and, in an extreme case, prevent it from arriving at the truth. As we have already shown it is of vital importance that Tribunals should discover the truth, for it may cause the gravest injustice to individuals and gravely damage the public interest if they do not do so. The only legal sanction to prevent the evidence from becoming contaminated lies in the law of contempt.

'32. We do not however accept the extreme view that it should be a contempt to publish any interview with a potential witness. On the other hand the overwhelming weight of evidence has been that any interview which can be proved to have been conducted with the deliberate intention of contaminating the evidence should be punishable as a contempt. We agree. It seems to us, however, that since it is so vitally important that evidence should not be contaminated anything said or done in relation to an interview or communication with a potential witness which is obviously likely to contaminate the evidence should also constitute a contempt. Under certain circumstances, the true nature of intention is by no means easy to define and may be the subject of much subtle argument. Indeed on some occasion the courts have been tempted to embark upon almost metaphysical speculations on this subject with unhappy results. We do not think that anyone who says or does anything in relation to an interview or communication with a potential witness which is obviously likely to contaminate the evidence has any just cause for complaint if this puts him in contempt – particularly having regard to the loopholes which, in practice, would be left in this branch of the law if intention were to be made the sole criterion. We recommend therefore that it should be a contempt if any person after a Tribunal is appointed under the Act of 1921 says or does anything or causes anything to be said or done, in relation to any evidence relevant to the subject matter of the Inquiry which is intended or obviously likely to alter, distort, destroy or withhold such evidence from the Tribunal. This we hope and believe would make the law fairer and certainly clearer than it is at present.

'33. It often happens in the courts that judges ask the Press in the interests of justice not to publish certain names or other details, particularly in infant cases. These requests are never ignored but are always faithfully observed although no question of contempt could arise. It would always be open to the chairman of a Tribunal in his discretion to make a request that no interview with certain named persons whom he regards as especially vulnerable should be published. We have no doubt that such a request would be complied with. There would certainly be no obligation to comply with it, but clearly anyone who ignored it would do so with the clear knowledge that he was treading on dangerous ground.

'34. We recognise that although our recommendation would still leave some uncertainty, it would at any rate make the law clearer than it is at present. It would be better for the Press, Television and Radio than the absolute ban on the publication of such interviews that up to now they have imposed on themselves out of a sense of responsibility and also in the belief that such publication would probably amount to contempt. Complete certainty in this sphere is possible only by adopting one of two alternatives, (1) an absolute ban on the publication of interviews with potential witnesses, or (2) giving carte blanche in respect of all such interviews and their publication. The first alternative might be unfair to the Press, Television and Radio although the majority of the Press witnesses we have heard do not think that it would. The second alternative, we are convinced, would be unjust to those vitally concerned in the result of the Inquiry and would accordingly be contrary to the public interest.'

Chapter Eleven

The Foreign Secretary's intervention

156 We come now to the intervention of the Foreign and Commonwealth Secretary, Sir Geoffrey Howe, QC. On the evening of
Tuesday, 26 April, Sir Geoffrey telephoned the Chairman of the
IBA, Lord Thomson of Monifieth, and asked that the showing
of 'Death on the Rock' should be postponed until after the
inquest. The Foreign Secretary gave as the principal reason for
his request the fear that the broadcast might prejudice the
inquest. We understand that the possibility of contamination was
not mentioned at that stage. Lord Thomson said in reply that he
would look into the matter. As a result of this conversation, the
IBA consulted Leading Counsel, David Kemp, QC, and
received the advice referred to in chapter Nine, paragraph 126.

157 Neither the fact nor the substance of the conversation between
the Foreign Secretary and Lord Thomson was made known to
Thames. Lord Thomson told us that he regarded the Foreign
Secretary's request as having been made in confidence, but in
any event he felt that it was a matter for himself and the IBA to
decide what the proper response to such a request should be.

158 On the morning of Thursday, 28 April, following the viewings
which had taken place at the IBA the previous day (see chapter
Five, paragraph 58), it was decided by the Chairman and
Director-General that the transmission of the programme
should go ahead as scheduled at 9:00 pm that evening on the full
ITV network. The Director of Television, David Glencross, was
instructed to telephone Sir Geoffrey Howe's Private Secretary
and notify him of the Authority's decision, saying that it had
been taken at the highest level and after taking legal advice. At
about noon, the Foreign Secretary himself telephoned the IBA
and, in the absence of the Chairman, spoke to Glencross. On

this occasion, Sir Geoffrey Howe, a former Solicitor-General, raised the issue of contamination, referred to the Salmon Report, and read out some extracts relating to contamination. Shortly thereafter, the FCO held a press conference at which the Foreign Secretary's unsuccessful dialogue with the IBA was made public. It was consequently not until the afternoon of the day of transmission that Thames became aware of the Government's concern.

159 In the light of the Foreign Secretary's further representations, the IBA immediately scrutinized the relevant parts of the Salmon Report and again consulted their legal advisers. Having done so, they concluded that his arguments ought not to prevail, for the following reasons:

(i) The programme had produced new witnesses for the inquest who might not otherwise have been available.

(ii) The programme did not set itself up as an alternative inquest or inquiry. It had volunteered all its information to the Gibraltar coroner.

(iii) At the time of the programme, no date for the inquest had been set.

(iv) It was clear that the broadcast of the programme in the United Kingdom would not constitute a contempt under the existing law.

(v) The effect of the Salmon Committee's recommendation was that any extension of the law of contempt should be limited to interviews or other material obtained or published with the deliberate intent or obvious likelihood of causing any relevant evidence to be altered, distorted, destroyed or withheld. The IBA's considered view was that the interviews with witnesses in 'Death on the Rock' did not fall into that category.

(vi) The Salmon Committee's recommendation was made in 1969. Under the Contempt of Court Act 1981, a publication can only incur strict liability for contempt if it creates 'a substantial risk that the course of justice ... will be seriously impeded or prejudiced.' In the IBA's opinion, the programme did not fall within that definition.

(vii) Because Gibraltar is a small community, the shootings were already likely to have been the subject of much public comment and discussion, even without the benefit of press and broadcasting coverage. There had been a great deal of local coverage in the Gibraltar press and on television, including eyewitness accounts, in the weeks between the shootings and the Thames programme. The Gibraltar authorities had made no move to prevent this. There had also been extensive coverage in the UK press, without comment from government or the law officers.

(viii) The programme was a legitimate piece of journalistic activity. It was not designed to usurp the function of the inquest, nor was it trying to set itself up as a quasilegal process.

160 Following the broadcast, there was an exchange of letters between the Foreign Secretary and Lord Thomson. The text of these letters is reprinted, with permission, at the end of this chapter. We do so not simply to put on record the reasons which were deployed in support of the request and its rejection, but to convey the tone of the exchanges which we regard as entirely creditable to both parties. The Foreign Secretary made it clear that there was no thought of challenging the constitutional independence of the broadcasting authorities. It was, he said, 'a matter of self-discipline by the broadcasters and of responsible judgement by the broadcasting authorities'. In his reply Lord Thomson claimed: 'The right of broadcasters and the press to examine events of major public concern is well established and should be preserved.' He also replied to the specific criticisms on the lines of the summary given in the previous paragraph.

161 The central fact in a dispute of this sort is that it is the IBA, as a public body established by statute, which has the responsibility

of deciding whether or not a programme should be broadcast. Parliament has laid down specific requirements which the IBA must satisfy itself have been met before it can allow any programme to be broadcast. Therefore, unless it is possible to say in any given case that the IBA has failed to give due consideration to the question whether those requirements have been met, or has decided that question in a way which is wholly unreasonable, it is tempting to conclude that further reflection is neither necessary, proper nor useful. That would, however, be a narrow attitude and out of sympathy with the spirit in which we have approached our Inquiry.

162 For reasons that are in part similar, but in part additional, to those put forward by the IBA, we have concluded that 'Death on the Rock' did not carry any real risk of prejudice or contamination. Nor have we found there were any legal impediments to the broadcast of the programme, or that the requirements of balance, fairness and impartiality demanded by the various statutory, contractual and conventional provisions to which we have referred earlier in this report (chapter Two, paragraphs 15–20) were infringed. Yet beyond the precise constraints of the law stand wider considerations.

163 One source of enlightenment is the European Convention on Human Rights and Fundamental Freedoms to which the United Kingdom subscribes. Article 10 states:

(1) Everyone has the right to freedom of expression. This right shall include freedom to hold opinions and to receive and impart information and ideas without interference by public authority and regardless of frontiers. This Article shall not prevent States from requiring the licensing of broadcasting, television or cinema enterprises.

(2) The exercise of these freedoms, since it carries with it duties and responsibilities, may be subject to such formalities, conditions, restrictions or penalties as are prescribed by law and are necessary in a democratic society in the interests of

national security, territorial integrity or public safety, for the prevention of disorder or crime, for the protection of health or morals, for the protection of the reputation or rights of others, for preventing the disclosure of information received in confidence, or for maintaining the authority and impartiality of the judiciary.

164 According to Lord Goff of Chieveley, the effect of Article 10 is to identify a fundamental right to freedom of expression which can only be restricted by such provisions of domestic law as are necessary. In his view, the jurisprudence of the European Court of Human Rights has established that the word 'necessary' implies the existence of a pressing social need and that 'interference with freedom of expression should be no more than is proportionate to the legitimate aim pursued' by that restriction: (*A–G* v. *Guardian Newspapers* (No 2) [1988] 3 WLR 776, 808). We do not think the language of the European Convention, or even its interpretation by a Lord of Appeal, is conclusive when applied to the issue we are considering. But we look on them as helpful signposts.

165 The tendency of English law is rather to prescribe restraints on liberty, and to provide remedies for wrongs, than to confer general rights. Thus the Contempt of Court Act 1981 and the Broadcasting Act 1981 impose defined restrictions on freedom of expression by broadcasters. If those restrictions are complied with, then wholly exceptional circumstances will be needed before it can be argued convincingly that, as a matter of judgement alone, a television programme should not be shown. Opinions about how that judgement should be exercised are unlikely to be unanimous. Conflicting interpretations will be argued with absolute conviction allowing little or no scope for compromise.

166 We believe it right that those who bear Ministerial responsibility for the conduct of British foreign policy, or who have departmental responsibility for the Armed Forces, should be free to

make the strongest possible representations whenever they believe that a television programme may be harmful to the public interest. Interventions will be more effective if they are sparing and backed up by reasoned arguments, as was the case in this instance. Equally, the broadcasting authority appointed by Parliament must be prepared to withstand pressure, however fierce and whatever the source; nor should it give way to political expediency. It has an obligation to use its own independent judgement to decide upon what is or is not broadcast. Its discretion, as we have shown, is not unqualified. But its responsibility is final. 'Sir Geoffrey Howe did his duty', said Lord Thomson, 'and I did mine.' (*Daily Telegraph* 28 December 1988).

Foreign and Commonwealth Office
London SW1A 2AH

From the Secretary of State   4 May 1988

Dear George

It may be helpful if I set out in writing the reasons which I gave to you and to David Glencross last week when requesting that broadcasting of the programme 'Death on the Rock' should be postponed until after the inquest in Gibraltar. There are important points of principle concerned, which must not be allowed to become buried beneath the media furore.

I have two concerns. The first is that there should be no improper influence arising from the broadcasting of the programme on the forthcoming inquest in Gibraltar, a dependent territory of the UK for whose administration I am responsible. As you no doubt know, despite your decision not to market the programme in Gibraltar itself, it was shown there on Super Channel and important parts of it were also shown on the television news before the Attorney General was able to obtain an injunction to prevent further screening. I do not think you should under-estimate the potential pressure which a programme of this kind may put on a jury or a court.

Secondly, there is a more general principle at stake. As a barrister in the Aberfan inquiry, I have had personal experience of the prejudicial effect which the irresponsible and partial presentation of 'evidence' on television can have on a judicial inquiry. The principles set out by Lord Salmon in his report on the law of contempt as it affects tribunals of inquiry are as relevant today as they were then. The key passage is:

'The Press, Television and Radio have always considered that once any type of tribunal has been appointed it is inappropriate for them to conduct anything in the nature of a parallel inquiry and they have never done so. We regard it as of the utmost importance that this restraint should continue to be exercised.'

I am enclosing a longer extract from the report which in my view is entirely relevant to your decision to allow the screening of 'Death on the Rock' before the inquest. You will remember that Sir Geoffrey Cox, former Editor and Chief Executive of ITN, was a member of the Commission which produced the report.

The dangers are clear, and so is the resulting responsibility laid upon the media. The dangers are the more real in the case of the television medium because the interviewing of witnesses is presented in a much more direct way than in the written press: there must be a serious risk of contaminating the evidence by establishing potential witnesses in advance of the hearing in public positions with all the attendant pressures which that produces. I need hardly say that there are particular risks if there is any question of payment to those who participate, though I do not know if that was the case in this instance.

Quite apart from this there is the added danger of editorial selections on which parts of interviews to broadcast affecting the interpretation of the evidence. According to press reports, there is already some dispute as to whether the edited version which was transmitted of the responses of one of those interviewed correctly reflected his views.

There is no question of the Government seeking to 'muzzle' the media. There is no thought of Ministers challenging the constitutional independence of the broadcasting authorities. It is a matter of self-discipline by the broadcasters and of responsible judgement by the broadcasting authorities. There is no doubt that the programme was highly relevant to the inquest which is expected to be held in the near future in Gibraltar, and which will be of great public interest and the subject of detailed public scrutiny. Furthermore, it directly affected the security forces of this country. I cannot think of a better example of a case where Lord Salmon's report applies.

I therefore must express my deep regret and serious disquiet that despite these arguments you should have felt able to proceed with the broadcast before the inquest had taken place.

Yours sincerely
Geoffrey

GEOFFREY HOWE

Baron Thomson of Monifieth PC

Note: Enclosed with the Foreign Secretary's letter were paragraphs 29, 30 and 31 of the Report of the Interdepartmental Committee of the Law of Contempt as it affects Tribunals of Inquiry (The Salmon Report).

INDEPENDENT BROADCASTING AUTHORITY

70 Brompton Road, London SW3 1EY
Tel: 01-584 7011 Telex: 24345

THE RT. HON. THE LORD THOMSON OF MONIFIETH, KT, PC
Chairman

By Hand   12th May 1988

Dear Geoffrey,

Thank you for your letter of 4th May following your request for us to postpone broadcasting the programme 'Death on the Rock'.

You expressed concern over two issues. The first was that there should be no improper influence on the jury in the forthcoming inquest in Gibraltar. The second concerned the possible contamination of evidence that in your view could arise from interviews with witnesses on television.

On the first issue, you will already be aware that the IBA and Thames Television took legal advice and were told there was no likelihood of transmission of the programme in the United Kingdom being held to be in contempt of court. No judicial proceedings are pending in the United Kingdom which could be prejudiced by the broadcast and all enquiries into the shooting are being conducted outside the jurisdiction of any British court.

The programme was withheld by Thames from transmission in Gibraltar itself, though extracts, not the whole programme, were shown on Super Channel news, which is produced by ITN and relayed on Gibraltar Television. ITN informed Gibraltar Television of this in advance and our enquiries show the station there then took its own legal advice before clearing the item for local transmission. This decision is of course a matter for the television authorities in Gibraltar and not for the IBA. However, most of the witnesses in the Thames programme had already given television interviews for local use.

With regard to your second concern about the possible contamination of evidence, you cite Lord Salmon's Report of 1969 on the law of contempt as it affects Tribunals of Inquiry. In our view, Lord Salmon's recommendations are not relevant to the decision taken by the Authority over this programme. There is to be no Tribunal of Inquiry in Gibraltar. The Salmon Report confined its comments solely to such Tribunals and recommended that the law of contempt should apply only from the date of the instrument appointing them. Indeed, Lord Salmon's Committee concluded that 'we do not consider that the law of contempt should apply as soon as the Government of the day has announced its intention of establishing a Tribunal of Inquiry. This we think would be giving too much power to the executive.' (Para. 24).

Furthermore, in the paragraph immediately after the ones you have cited from the section dealing with contamination of evidence, the Salmon Committee said it did not accept what it called 'the extreme view' that once a Tribunal had been appointed it should be a contempt to publish any interviews with potential witnesses. It recommended instead that contempt should be restricted to anything said or done with the deliberate intent or obvious likelihood that it would lead to any relevant evidence being altered, distorted, destroyed or withheld.

I cannot accept the argument that the interviews transmitted in 'Death on the Rock' fall into that category. On the contrary, the programme uncovered new evidence and potential witnesses who may not otherwise have been available to the inquest.

Apart from the importance of avoiding contempt, the issues as we see them relate to free speech and free enquiry which underpin individual liberty in a democracy. The right of broadcasters and the press to examine events of major public concern is well established and should be preserved. In the last year alone the enquiries of the media and their interviews with eye-witnesses have helped to inform the public about the circumstances surrounding such events as the Zeebrugge ferry disaster, the King's Cross fire, the shootings at Hungerford, the Remembrance Day massacre at Enniskillen, and the brutal murders at the Andersonstown funeral – all of them controversial. In all these cases inquests have been held and in some cases public enquiries have also been set up without any suggestion that previous interviews with witnesses on television or in the press have interfered with the course of justice.

I am sorry that you and I, from our different standpoints, should have come to different conclusions about the Thames programme. I recognise that you were fully entitled to make your concerns known to us. However, I believe that the decision I made for the IBA, which my colleagues have unanimously endorsed, to allow the broadcast to go ahead was the right one in all the circumstances; and I am glad to see that this has not been questioned by such an eminent judge as Lord Scarman (letter in The Times of Monday, 9th May) who has himself presided over more than one major Tribunal of Inquiry.

Yours sincerely

George

The Rt. Hon. Sir Geoffrey Howe, QC, MP,
Secretary of State,
Foreign and Commonwealth Office,
Downing Street,
London, SW1A 2AL.

Chapter Twelve

'Death on the Rock': a child of its time

167 Our terms of reference did not invite us to make any recommendations, nor are we tempted to offer any. Our remit was to inquire into the making and screening of 'Death on the Rock' and this report is the outcome of three months' work. Rather than attempting to summarize the detailed conclusions which are contained in the preceding chapters of narrative, we have chosen to bring our task to finality with some reflections on the implications of our findings. Although this may seem an unusual course it is, we believe, consistent with the way in which we have approached an unusual, indeed unprecedented, assignment. Carefully weighed as they have been, the conclusions we have reached are no more important than the reasoning which lies behind them. We do not want to risk diverting the reader's attention and understanding by providing a short cut via a compressed recital of findings at the end.

168 It will have become evident from a reading of the report that we do not see ourselves as adjudicating upon the controversial issues of fact to which the shootings gave rise. We express no opinion on the validity of the differing explanations that have been put forward. Our stance has been to probe and dissect the anatomy of a single television current affairs programme: its antecedents, the way it was made, its true meaning and effect, the criticisms it attracted, and the decision to broadcast despite the Government's request that it be postponed.

169 As the Inquiry progressed, we became increasingly conscious that to subject any programme to such a very detailed scrutiny several months after it had been screened would be likely to reveal some inaccuracies, inconsistencies or lapses in judgement. Yet of its very nature television journalism, like newspaper

reporting, does not depend on absolute accuracy for its validity.
Journalists are often writing against the clock, sometimes (as in
this case) pursuing inquiries of undoubted public importance,
but without the co-operation of some or all of the directly
interested parties. They can only work with the sources which
are available at the time and cannot be expected to acquiesce in
treating certain subjects as being put out of bounds whenever
those in authority consider it to be inappropriate or irresponsible
for potentially embarrassing or inconvenient questions to be
asked. The relatively unrestricted opportunities for investigation
which the British print and broadcast media enjoy are only
earned, however, if what is known of the other side, be it an
official policy or a private interest, is fairly put before the public.

170   How did 'Death on the Rock' measure up to this standard? A
short extract from the Foreign Secretary's statement to the
House of Commons on 7 March 1988 was included in the
programme and it was made clear in the commentary that the
Ministry of Defence was not prepared to comment until the
inquest. This reservation was repeated in the closing link by
Jonathan Dimbleby in the studio after the end of the film (see
chapter Four, page 68). Colonel Styles was engaged as a consultant in his personal and business capacity and never claimed to
represent the interests of the Armed Forces. Nor was he
presented in that light on the programme. But, because of his
distinguished military background and specialist knowledge of
bombing incidents and counter-terrorism, his participation
helped to achieve the editorial balance expected by the IBA in all
current affairs programmes. The same can be said of Mr Carman's contribution.

171   We have explained in chapter Five that an analysis of the content
of the programme has led us to the conclusion that taken as a
whole 'Death on the Rock' did not offend against the due
impartiality requirements of the IBA and the Broadcasting Act
1981. In paragraph 50 we find that the true meaning and effect
of the programme was that it pointed towards one possible

explanation of the shootings, namely that the deceased might have been unlawfully killed. This conclusion falls well short of the criticism that in effect the programme had posed the single question whether the terrorists had been executed as part of a deliberate plot, and then answered it in the affirmative. But we are aware that to some readers of this report the distinction may seem a fine one, which is another reason for urging a study of the arguments which we offer to support it.

172 It may be it was the thoroughness with which the programme was produced, and the vividness with which it was presented, that made 'Death on the Rock' a lightning conductor for the intense feelings that the Gibraltar shootings evoked in the minds of the British public. It was evident from Parliament and the press that attitudes were deeply divided. Some people felt that in countering the IRA's brutal campaign of violence, which in this instance could only have resulted in many civilian as well as military casualties, the security forces were fully entitled to take such measures as were necessary to protect the people of Gibraltar and the soldiers of the Royal Anglian Regiment from planned assassination. Others, while similarly abhorring the IRA's objectives and tactics, were disturbed about the implications of any actions by the security forces, whether in Northern Ireland or elsewhere, which fell outside the specific limitations of the rule of law by which they are bound. The conflict was essentially one of divergent personal attitudes and values rather than of party political divisions. Some reactions were inchoate, instinctive rather than certain; others were forthright and passionate. Sentiments of patriotism and loyalty towards the Armed Forces, the police and the security services in the highly dangerous and unpleasant duties they are called upon to perform jostled with doubts prompted by conscience.

173 Hazardous though it is to get close to a lightning conductor, even after the storm has passed, we can take heart from the fact that such strongly conflicting views were widely and eloquently voiced on an issue of profound public importance. There

seemed no room for apathy or lack of interest in what had happened in Gibraltar, nor was there any apparent inhibition on the advocacy of contrasting opinions. Diverse values freely expressed are unmistakable marks of a free society. It does not always make for a comfortable or popular life for those who have unleashed powerful forces they may not have anticipated but, as Lord Thomson remarked in a telling quotation included in chapter Two (paragraph 22), broadcast journalists must not be too sensitive towards criticism of their work or function.

174 We advance the proposition that 'Death on the Rock' reflected the virtues and limitations of television journalism in the late Eighties. The paradox is that while taken overall the programme fulfilled the requirements of a complex regulatory system, its transmission outraged a section of the population at large as well as provoking bitter criticism in Parliament and the press. If 'Death on the Rock' has taken on any distinctive role as we have lived with it throughout our Inquiry, it represents to us a child of its time, capable of being troublesome and valued simultaneously. The programme-makers were experienced, painstaking and persistent. They did not bribe, bully or misrepresent those who took part. The programme was trenchant and avoided triviality. Despite the various criticisms which we have noted in our report, we accept that those who made it were acting in good faith and without ulterior motives.

175 Yet we have found that the effect of the programme went beyond its stated intention of laying before the viewers certain evidence giving rise to questions that deserved to be examined by an authoritative tribunal such as a judicial inquiry (chapter Five, paragraphs 48–51). The suggestion that the terrorists might have been unlawfully killed was enough to offend those in the viewing public who saw in the programme a subversive and unfair attack on the security forces when they were unable to give their side of the story. The content of the programme was demonstrably unsympathetic towards the IRA in its orientation (chapter Three, paragraph 41). Nevertheless some of these

viewers found it lacking in identification with the objectives of the security forces. Exactly the same criticism had been made of media coverage at the time of the Falklands War. While the public mood is notoriously difficult to interpret there are sufficient indications that 'Death on the Rock' was out of step with a substantial body of national opinion. Others, of course, took a contrary view and spoke up accordingly.

176 We cannot ignore the realization that it was the alienated rather than the satisfied voices which brought about the establishment of our Inquiry in October 1988. Whether such a state of affairs is seen as a matter of concern, or simply as the price of independence, is another and larger question. We leave our report with one final reflection. Whatever view is taken of the state of public opinion and the legitimacy of Government intervention, the making and screening of 'Death on the Rock' proved that freedom of expression can prevail in the most extensive, and the most immediate, of all the means of mass communication.

[signed]   WINDLESHAM

[signed]   RICHARD RAMPTON

19 January 1989